Fun & Fearless Leadership

Leadership is fire

I owe most of who I am to my mother, who raised me to be free.

Foreword

This is a leadership book, not a technical management text, and it's for everyone looking to improve their understanding of themselves, of others and their ability to get things done. I draw most of my experience from IT, but this is not an industry-specific book, it's plain English. There is an order to the steps, especially if you want to apply them in a team, but they don't necessarily have to be read sequentially. You can jump back and forth if that's your style. There will be some backreferences, but not too many.

Throughout the entire experience, I am going to treat you like an adult. Many of the techniques and attitudes I describe are not the safest possible path you could take in any given situation, but this is not a book about maximizing safety. I aim to liberate and to empower you to do things you never thought you could, and I am writing this book as a sharp instrument, one that you can use to great effect, but you could also cut yourself with if you're not careful. This is nothing extraordinary, such is all life when fully lived. I trust you will learn from your mistakes, get up when you fall and try again. The difficult road is the most rewarding, and I bet you are, even if you don't feel like it, ready.

Contents

You've got to care 1
Humility 3
Crows in cities 3
Leadership is fire 9
    Obsession 9
    In defense of business 13
    Ideological leadership 18
    Stoic leadership 22
    The new angels 24
The Fun & Fearless System of Leadership 25
    Who is the system for? 25
    It's hard, but you can do it 28
Step 1: A long, hard look in the mirror 31
    Scorpions and marshmallows 31
    What's your cheetah skill? 36
    Develop your Mental Sherlock 40
    Learning & unlearning 45
    Dealing with your demons 48
    Personality tests - worth it? 52
Step 2: Start strong, end well 54
    The first day 54
    Do it early, keep moving, stop the focus erosion 55
    Be fearless 58
    Understand your new job 59

- Don't shave that yak 60
- Giving up too early 61
- Stopping too late 63
- Domesticated failure and wild failure 66
- Step 3: The miracle of compassionate radical honesty 71
  - Caring effectively 71
  - Stone age hardware 75
  - What Radical Honesty is and isn't 79
  - The doctor syndrome 82
  - The one operating principles of Radical Honesty 82
  - Cultural differences 83
  - Death by politeness 88
  - What transparency is and isn't 91
  - Compassion 92
  - When and how to apologize 96
  - The right kind of stubbornness 98
  - Earning the right 99
- Step 4: Get the right people 100
  - Hire better 100
  - Advanced intuition 107
  - Promote better 108
  - Fire better 111
  - Your reputation 112
  - Useful networking 112
- Step 5: Culture 114
  - What is culture 114

Why culture matters 116
Deterministic and free market 117
Professional monogamy 119
The official canon and the fan stories 122
Zombie culture is worse than no culture 123
Little Red Riding Hood and a safe culture 125
Winners write the history books 126
Trying too hard 127
Nothing kills faster than pink elephants 129
The criticality of public displays 131
Measurements 132
Minimal rules 139
Why you can't have your cake and eat it too 142
Stand for something obvious and burn all bridges 144
Politics and bad apples 145
Culture tools 147

Step 6: Building fluent teams 148
Fluent teams 148
Bad Teams 148
Any team needs three things 151
Safety 152
CRH in the team 155
Getting personal 157
Who's taking the puppy home? 159
The Journey 161
Decisions: Consensus vs leader, slow vs fast, facts vs guts 164

    Suffocating authority vs liberating authority 167
    Dishonest relationships 169
    A habit of mental poverty 170
    The neat car syndrome 171
    Drive & motivation 172
    Performance 180
    Changing hearts and minds 192
    Extraordinary teams in average locations? 193
Step 7: The magic 195
    You don't have a lot of time 195
    Lead everything 196
    Don't be a good worker 198
    Ultimate professional relationships 199
    Legacy 200
The time to be an optimist is now 203

v1.0 29.09.18

You've got to care

I have a massive issue with authority and an even bigger one with conformity. When I decided, in my mid-twenties, to stop being an arrogant, people avoiding, interaction repelling uber-geek with nothing but contempt for human society and all its norms, I knew at the same time that I wasn't about to discover the wisdom of a two bedroom apartment, a mortgage, a family and the routine of the 9 to 5, spiked with a couple of vacations a year enjoying Bulgaria's all-inclusive seaside resorts, which I still view as a version of hell (nothing personal, Bulgaria, it's not you, it's me).

Growing up, there was something suffocating around me, like an ever-present retched fog, in the way in which most of my teachers taught, in the way in which people spoke, in the way in which the world worked. With precious few exceptions, the only kind of freedom I found was in books, in my imagination, in solitude. It wasn't, as you might imagine, a state of sadness or torment, from the contrary, I found it natural to rebel and detach, comfortable and happy in my solitude, enjoying my, real or imagined, exceptionalism. I created my own bubble, removed from the world around me, helped by a vivid imagination and a natural inclination to reading. I occasionally confronted a teacher on some point or another, sometimes cared, briefly, about current events, but generally, I just lived in my own head, treating the world with the indifference and disdain worthy of a Swedish film director. I was stubborn, arrogant, critical, avid for information, a voracious learner, of what I wanted and only of what I wanted, intellectually and emotionally independent from as young of an age as I can remember. What I was not was a leader, although I had many of the qualities that would have made me one, and the reason I was not a leader was that I did not care for the world around me. I literally cried when I first read about Caesar's assassination and I wept all night long on New Year's Eve in 1988, because I was 8 years world, the year of '88 was ending, and I loved the number 8, and when again were there going to be so many 8's in my life? As I put my heart and soul into these abstract concerns, and many others like them, I did not have the interest to know the names of my neighbors, living meters from me, on the same flight of stairs, in the same apartment block, who I passed by, daily, for years, without greeting, without looking at them.

I didn't care. The reasons don't really matter. Maybe I didn't care because I knew I wouldn't be in that city for long, that my life was going to be somewhere else, or maybe I just was that way as a kid, or maybe I was afraid of something, or maybe I just really liked, like I still do, my privacy. It doesn't matter why, but because I didn't care, I didn't lead, I wasn't interested, I wasn't involved.

You can't be a leader if you don't care. You can be many other things, you can be a genius, you can be an expert, you can be a manager, but you can't be a leader. Before any skills, before anything else, leadership is caring about something enough to put yourself out there, to reach, to step up, to take a chance. It's that something that compels you to do the right thing and get the job done, even when no one is looking, and especially when you have something to lose. You can fake it for a while, but only for a while.

As soon as I started to care, I started to lead. I wasn't good at first, but the intention was there almost immediately. It's simple to understand why: when you care you know that you have to make things better, and when you are serious about what that means, you realize that you have to work with others, together, because you can do more than on your own. The most impactful way of working with others is to lead, and by that I don't necessarily mean to take charge, to be the boss, as we'll see throughout this book.

Leadership is a manifestation of giving a damn, and it's a sophisticated manifestation because it requires courage, self-awareness and a whole host of skills, some more specific than others.

I started giving a damn when I realized that the things I took for granted were anything but, and ever since I've been, with ups and downs, with leaps and setbacks, through pleasure and pain, getting braver and getting better. This is not because I am unique in any way, this is how things work: determination and persistence improve us. This book is my story of getting from there to here, but, more importantly, it's my way of passing on what I've learned, of helping you find the truth of what you care about, the courage to dedicate yourself to it and the many techniques, lessons and anecdotes that will give you a complete, realistic and effective toolset to succeed, and do it your way. The only thing you must absolutely do is care, and no one else can do that for you.

Humility

As I write this book, I am humbled by three things. The miracle of reality, the impossible challenge of putting all the nuances of what I see, think and feel in writing, it humbles me. The spirit, courage and achievements of the many amazing professionals I've had the chance to work with, it humbles me as well. The brilliance of amazing books I wish I could have written, and I am grateful to have read, it also humbles me.

Crows in cities

I read a fascinating article once on how crows in cities evolve new behaviors so much faster than crows in the wild, in response to the wider array of both danger and opportunity they face in their city life.

Traditional leadership practice has evolved in its natural environment of well-developed countries, stable economies, big business, generally protestant old boy networks, slowly and steadily. Crows in the field. I on the other hand come from the edge of the world, 10 miles from the Eastern border of the European Union, ex-communist state, ex disaster, all digital, all improv. I come from the scrapyard. I had no history and no expectations. Crow in a city, out of my natural environment, shaped by strange circumstances. I dived into the deep end of leadership with no help in the beginning, with a healthy disdain for all forms of authority, learned my lessons my way, the hard way, hungry for knowledge, never satiated, I came to a simple conclusion: leadership is movement. Leadership is not made out of marble. Leadership is fire.

I am not here to preach responsibility. I am not here to teach you how to be gentle and liked, this is not a book about making friends. And I'm definitely not here to teach you how to be a mildly successful, predictable middle manager. I am not going to pour my soul into this so the best you do with it is incrementally improve your powerpoint game. You wanna be a rocknrolla? This is the book for you. Are you afraid to make some noise, to stop trying to please everyone? Then this book is going to scare you, but maybe that's exactly what you need.

Fun & Fearless is a system of effective and satisfying leadership behaviors. I write about how you can take control of yourself and your situation and employ your talents, determination and hard work towards change. Leadership is all about change. Leaders exist to change something, to fix a problem, to make something new, to make something better. Caretakers are content to see things moving along in the general intended direction. Caretakers and leaders are two different things. I am not interested in caretakers.

I draw my lessons from my life and my experience: software developer, then software architect, manager in IT companies, consultant, entrepreneur. The bulk of my career has happened here in Iași, Romania, where I've been part of the amazing growth of the local IT industry, from a few hundred people in the early 2000's to close to 20.000 now. I've worked in outsourcing, in product development, as a consultant, in projects small and large, with teams small and large, with clients small and large, from different countries.

I also draw my lessons from the experience of my friends, colleagues, partners and clients, who I've been lucky enough to work with, to see working and to share time with. I also learned from the best literature in business, psychology, sociology and more, as no leader can be complete without educating himself on things outside of what he directly sees and experiences. The practicality and viscerality of what I've done myself, of what I've seen and touched, combined with the inspiring stories of others.

I write out of Romania, a country still better known in some places for its depressing communist era architecture, packs of stray dogs and severe poverty. A country of megalomaniac projects of a crazed dictator we killed on Christmas day in 1989, a country of inefficient industry, of dysfunctional work ethic, an obedient society beaten into being content to keep its head down and survive. What leadership lessons can possibly come out of here? This is no Silicon Valley, this is no London, this is not a place where you'd imagine a decent car service operating. What gives?

I'll tell you what gives. For one, that is not my Romania. Yes, all of that is true, and much of this country is still stuck there, in its head if nothing else, but I have less in common with that traditional Romania than I have with the Marvel Cinematic Universe, and I'm not even a hardcore MCU fan. I wasn't culturally connected, I wasn't involved, I did not take my cues from there, I had no models there, it was a physical location in which I existed and nothing else. I was a weird kid, removed, disconnected, socially awkward, distant, arrogant, living in my mind, and all that saved me from contamination. My family was of very modest means and that saved me from entitlement. Systems weren't working and that gave me opportunities that would, today, be impossible. Teachers would get arrested for the kind of free range and autonomy they allowed me back then. Several laws would have to be broken today, including child labor laws, if some kid somewhere in some school would be let and asked to do what I was let and asked to do. I'm not defending that world as a whole, I'm not saying it was a good world, but what I am saying is that I had an extraordinary environment to develop myself in, remarkable conditions that allowed me unique learning opportunities, and I'm grateful for that.

My city today is a wonderful, vibrant and happening place, and it's all because of IT. The story of how the IT industry in Iași came to be from nothing to what it is today is, in a sense, the story of kids left to our own devices, with no adult supervision. Grownups walked on the same streets and shopped at the same stores as us, but they inhabited a different world. Authorities had nothing to do with it, they were clueless to what was happening under their noses for a decade if not more. Universities didn't lead, universities followed, and mostly still do. It's no exaggeration to say that IT made the part of Romania that is modern, prosperous and ambitious. We have the fastest broadband in the whole western world and it started in the 90s from the uncoordinated initiatives of thousands of small entrepreneurs that wired the apartment blocks they lived in, bought one internet subscription, then prohibitively expensive, pieced it out and resold it to their neighbors, through the improvised wiring they did, all unregulated, all off the books. When this later consolidated, it was the foundation for what we have now. When Google made huge press in 2011 with their gigabit fiber service and made a, I thought, sad show, by asking cities to compete for the pilot, it was barely news over here. We had fiber to our doors by then and paid 15$ a month for our gigabit connection. This new Romania is concentrated in a handful of cities, out of which my city, Iași, pronounced Yash, is among the four most important ones.

The first small IT businesses were what we called "apartment companies". 5-10 employees strong, they would rent an apartment and would provide the most rudimentary kind of outsourcing services. They used apartments because they didn't need more and couldn't afford it, but also because we had no office buildings to speak of. They paid shit salaries, survival level, and routinely were late in doing that by weeks, or months. Work was exhausting, 12 hour long days, weekends, unpaid overtime, no choice, no rights, no pampering, a world away from today's glass and steel buildings with PlayStation equipped offices with organic, locally grown apples freely supplied. Slowly, these companies grew, multinationals came, the standards were raised, demand grew exponentially and a full ecosystem developed around it.

We did it in a world that was not in the slightest ready for us: a post-communist society with no flair for business, with no leadership models whatsoever, not in traditional business nor in public life, with parents and teachers that, with precious few exceptions, did not understand what we were doing. It is telling that IT burst into the collective consciousness in Iași as recently as 2014-2015, when it became the largest export of the this most populous county of Romania, overtaking agriculture. Suddenly, mainstream newspapers, officials and everyone else were all on us, talking about the knowledge economy, babbling about smart cities and whatnot, organizing lame conferences, hungry for our money and our votes.

Oily salesmen came in to tell us how "the real world" works. Whole sectors of service industries, from hip pubs to luxury salons to organic cookies advertised to and targeted the very well paid IT professionals.

And so, along with the good also crept in the bullshit and not all is shiny in this wonderland of ours.

What was once the joy of working in small teams in love with the code is now slowly becoming corporate drudgery that no amount of bean bags, table tennis, free fruit and back rubs at your desk can wipe away. What were once brave teams that did not think much about throwing away the code and starting afresh is now a layer of middle managers pressured from below by increasing expectations of increasingly entitled talent and from above by the averaging tendencies of all bureaucracies, especially outsourcing ones. An entire generation is hurling towards midlife crisis having lost its spirit, having retreated from the communities and the wee hours of morning debates into paying monthly installments for their houses and finding their sole outlets for joy in growing their own little patch of tomatoes in their backyards. The young ones are coming into an industry that while immensely richer, bigger and in many ways more impressive than back in the day, it is decidedly less fearless and not as brilliantly inspiring as it could, and as it deserves to be.

We need a better way, a breakthrough. We need leadership. It's as simple as that. And yes, we've been getting leadership lessons, the traditional kind. It helped, in the beginning, it filled in basics gaps we had, but fundamentally, it's not working. Their kind of leadership is for a world patiently built by families, brick by brick, linearly, dinner together after a hard day's work. The world I'm looking at is exponential, non intuitive, complex beyond easy understanding, scary in many ways, thrilling in others. Humanity is different here, brothers break bread in new ways, cause and effect work in unfamiliar fashion. This is no place and no time for brick by brick leadership. This is the time for the great abyss and the incredible heights.

My goal is to bring back the Fun and The Fearless, adapted for the new reality, ready for the future. This weird ecosystem that this city has been for me, like one of those isolated islands where species evolve in ways not found anywhere else, tiny dinosaurs and giant caterpillars, has been the perfect accelerator allowing me to see an entire industry grow in front of my eyes, having been in it every step of the way, and it has taught me more than I could have ever learned in the same amount of time in an established, mature city somewhere in an established, mature country. I would have been less if I had worked all my career so far in London, or New York or wherever. More in other ways, yes, but less in those that make me different, that make this place special, that make this book something worth reading if you're doing in IT in Iași, in Cluj, Warsaw, Berlin, Stockholm or anywhere else. This has been a remarkable context.

My book is for all concentrations of creative work where leadership needs to be fresh and meaningful, but it's constantly being pulled by uniforming forces into becoming predictable and boring. I'm not talking about leadership as a kind of duty or a sort of societal role, that's too constraining for me and too constraining for the future that we need to shape. I'm looking at leadership as a set of change generating behaviors that necessarily involve some degree of interaction with others, and these behaviors are a choice. You choose to engage in them for the sake of some change you want to see done, be it something built, or something protected. Once you engage, your chances of success are going to be improved by acting in certain ways. This is what this book is about: effectively and bravely engaging in leadership behaviors towards something you deeply care for.

Fairweather captains will middle manage all day long in corporations and their employers are going to tell them they're doing a good job and are going to give them raises, because they need them, and good enough is good enough. When the water retreats, as Warren Buffets brilliantly put it, we'll get to see who's been swimming butt naked all this time, and good enough ain't going to be good enough anymore.

Leadership is fire

Obsession

Vaslui in the 90's was about as bad as a place can get without becoming a certified tragedy. At times the poorest city in all of non ex-Soviet Europe, and not far from it even now, the town of Vaslui had seen its population quadruple in 40 years of communism, up to a high of 80.000 in the 1992 census. When the regime fell and the factories with it, like dominoes, one after another, half the reason for this city to exist went away as well. Poverty, despair, mass migration and accelerated degradation of infrastructure and government at all levels quickly followed. My childhood memories are of kids, me among them, ganging up, going to the town's edge, climbing the huge pipes through which hot water used to run, twice a week, now not used anymore, stripping away the massive sheets of rusting metal wrapped around them, put there to hold the insulation, taking them with us, carrying them on our backs and shaping them into rectangular boats, which we then spent our days on, crossing the Bârlad river back and forth. We had fleets of these things, dozens. When we got tired and hungry after a hard day of boating, we went into the train station, climbed over fences, went up into the carriages, improvised bags out of our t-shirts and filled them with raw soybeans which we then roasted at campfires we made, sat around and ate on the banks of the same river we had navigated earlier, late into the night, sucked on by the mosquito swarms and serenaded by thousands of frogs croaking all night long. Our parents knew, the river ran through the town, in front of the apartment blocks, under their eyes, they saw out fires from their kitchen windows, but that was normal back then and they didn't care. They were the people that did not think twice about sacrificing a pig for Christmas, if they were lucky to get one, in front of the apartment building, butchering and smoking it there, street side. They were also the people that colonized every little patch of dirt in between the gray cement buildings, parceled it out and grew cabbage and carrots, because money was tight, very tight, and people had to eat. Urban gardens are a hipster dream these days, but we did it because we had to.

That's where I grew up. At the age of 15, when I finished general school and it was time to move to high school, I ended up in informatics, at the Ștefan Procopiu High School, although I don't remember why and how. It was the second most desirable high school out of the 4 in town, I remember that, but why I chose it, I don't recall. I didn't have a computer at home, that was an unheard-of luxury. I had, rarely, touched computers at my mother's workplace, I liked it, but there was no continuity there, it wasn't like I was thinking of computers every day. By that time, I had grown secluded and wasn't really going outside anymore to play with the other kids. Instead, I was spending most of my time watching the Discovery Channel, especially history and war documentaries, reading and rereading the few books we had at home, imagining worlds. I had already developed a passion for staying up late fantasizing and obsessing about all kinds of intellectual pursuits, and, not surprisingly, I had also already learned to hate mornings. While tempered by the constraints of adulthood, this is still true today and I do my best to avoid any kind of responsibility before 9 AM at the absolute earliest. Back to 1995 in Vaslui, I don't remember why, but I went to the computers high school and I got into the first of the two informatics classes, the G, the flagship.

This is when my career began, at the age of 15, when, with no plan and no intention, with no vision or purpose about the future, with no understanding of life, I wandered into the Ștefan Procopiu High School in Vaslui, the informatics class, and I discovered computers, and they changed my life completely, more than any other thing I ever did.

Writing this, I realize I was already myself even then. My most important quality, obsession, defined my childhood, my teens, my youth and is still my main drive today.

Obsession is why there was nothing strange to me about suddenly deciding to wait every day after school in front of the building that hosted the computer laboratories. My high school had a very well-equipped lab, with 20-30 PCs, something that was extraordinarily rare in Romania at that time. It was, thanks to a foreign grant, one of the best equipped high schools in the country. As soon as I stepped into it for my first lab class in my first week of high school, I was hooked at first sight and I don't remember another time in my life where I felt quite as high as an exhilarating feeling than what I felt sitting down for the first time in front of that big, clunky, mechanical IBM keyboard attached to a 286 and typing my first commands in MS-DOS, staring into that bulbous monitor, eyes glued to the cursor blinking, fixated and transformed by every letter that I made appear, like watching dancing green flames that I was willing into existence. I wish to every one of you reading this book at least one moment of such pure single-minded rapture in your lives. I've had several so far and I wouldn't trade them for all the money in the world. Such intensity and joy are impossible to recreate on cue even in the most spectacular circumstances and the most spectacular locations. Unicorn seconds, one in a million, one in a billion.

Why was I waiting in front of the lab building? Because I needed, I craved, I had to have access after-hours to the computers, and I was waiting for the head teacher to pass by and ask for it. Some days I begged, some days I tried to be more composed, some days I probably teared up. I didn't know what I was doing, but I did it until it worked and after a couple of weeks I was in. I was lucky. They had just gotten the computers, but there was nobody to set them up, clean them up, reinstall the software when it needed to, fix them when they broke. The teachers didn't have the time, the knowledge, or the inclination to do it, so an unwritten pact was struck between us and them: 3-4 of us kids would be allowed into the labs whenever we wanted, after hours, on weekends, during vacations, and in exchange we'd take care of the computers, the servers, the student accounts, the network, everything. We'd also get to not go to any of the 10-12 hours a week we had of various informatics related classes, and all the teachers would give us 10's by default, in our absence. Wouldn't have helped to be there anyway, as we were about to learn by doing exponentially more and faster than our colleagues were learning by talking. For the next four years of my life, every day after classes, sometimes until midnight, sometimes later, almost every weekend, through winter and summer breaks, we were there, for days at a time even. We would eat biscuits and sleep on chairs and not go home from Friday until Sunday. We were totally unsupervised, by ourselves in a building on the side of the high school grounds, for days on end. Yes, we sometimes drank a bit and yes, some other times we played some games or downloaded a few porn pics (dial up internet wasn't up to downloading movies; our first mp3 took 4 hours to get, and it was Ricky Martin, for reasons out of my control). What's remarkable, or maybe not, is that we spent 90% of that time, which we could have used for anything we wanted whatsoever, with no consequences to consider, we spent it learning: installing and configuring different flavors of Linux, writing scripts, configuring networks, trying to hack things, learning programming languages, playing pranks on each other, like when I changed, re-compiled and re-installed a friend's ssh daemon so when I telneted to 22 and typed a certain word, his computer rebooted. I still giggle remembering him, to my right, cursing and trying to figure out what was happening.

I owe so much to the head teacher. She was never my teacher in a classroom, but that's not important, because she let me in and she trusted me, and others, and she made it all possible.

But even then, obsession was nothing new for me. When I was 10, or less, I was watching history documentaries for hours and then I wrote constitutions and drew maps for imaginary countries, and then spend a couple of months creating and documenting a history for that world: who did what, who fought who, how did it end. I did this 5 or 6 times over, 5 or 6 worlds. I read the Three Musketeers 13 times and I read Amadis of Gaul 14 times over, and that's one boring book to read even once, but back then I was fascinated by it. I had a couple of intensely religious years, reading the works of obscure saints, praying for hours every evening on my knees, by the bed, visiting a monastery for three days at one time, sleeping in a dormitory with a dozen other pilgrims. That's where I bought a booklet explaining why AC/DC and Metallica were the work of the devil, because of the horn sign and AC/DC coming from Anti Christ / Death to Christ. I believed it then and it gave me the chills. Fortunately for me, once I got into computers, Jesus didn't stand a chance. Software and hardware captivated me completely and there was no room for any other obsession. I never decided to stop believing, I just did, and I didn't even realize when it happened, it was so quick and complete, in a matter of weeks all the religion in me shriveled away at the sight of bits and bytes. Funny enough, couple of years later, Metallica was the first band I really could call myself a fan of and, to this day, one of the few live acts I made the time to go to.

Obsession never left me and it's my most important asset. All my worthwhile achievements come from obsession. If there's anything I regret, I regret the few years where I tried to be the kind of grownup that's balanced and seeks equilibrium and does a bit of this and a bit of that. Bollocks. More than a trait, more than a skill, more than a strategy, obsession is me. I am half a man without my obsessions, and not my better half.

In defense of business

Fast forward two decades and a bit to right now and let's talk business.

What is the point of business? In an existential sense, there is no "point" to anything. Business is the natural, unavoidable consequence of a free market where people are allowed to trade, and when these conditions are met, business emerges and exists, just as new kinds of plants and animals evolve and exist in life supporting ecosystems. On a personal level however, what is the point of business for each of us? Why do we join, admire, why do we start and invest in companies? Yes, we do it to make a living, but beyond that, what else is there?

I believe we do it because business is the greatest change agent in the world. More than governments, more than armies, more than anything else, business builds the world we live in. Business is the great engine that feeds on opportunity, knowledge, capital, scientific discoveries, cultural zeitgeist and makes products out of them, products that we then build our existence on, and in the process of doing so, generate more opportunity, knowledge, capital, scientific discoveries and cultural zeitgeist. If you want to change the world and make it better, more often than not, the most effective way to go about it is to start or join a successful business.

If we start or join a company that is aligned with our vision of the world, what is that company supposed to look like? There is no one right answer, and that is the beauty of the free market, but I will give you my answer, and my style of leadership is derived from it.

I respect and admire stable businesses, such as the Kongō Gumi, which was, until 2006, the oldest continuously run, and family owned to boot, business in the world, tracing its origins to at least 578 AD. It was a Japanese construction company, specialized in Buddhist temples. But as much as I am awed by such businesses, I am not excited by them and I would not invest my time in building a stable, family run, millennia and a half construction company.

I also have little excitement, and not that much awe either for the slumbering bureaucracies of the world. The ossified banks, the sleepwalking IT giants of days past. I have even less interest in those businesses that have long lost their creative engine and are hanging on because only because of exclusive access to some limited resource or another, like an oil field or some state sponsored monopoly of some sort. I like dynamic markets, where the cost of entry is low, and the ability to compete is limited only by your competence and the skills of your competitors.

For me, business is an agent of change, not one of stability and definitely not one of entitlement. When I tell people I like Tesla, they sometimes tell me that Tesla is not a stable company. To that, I reply, Great! The world doesn't need another Skoda, predictability delivering predictable cars in a polite way. We have all the Skoda we can ever want or need in our lives. If Tesla were to disappear tomorrow, it has still done more for us than most other companies in a century, and it has definitely inspired us more.

I can respect tradition, sometimes even like it, but what I like even more is breaking tradition and bringing in new ways of seeing things. I have two Revolut cards in my wallet not because I hate banks, I've worked with banks, there are some great people in banks, but because banks are big and old and Revolut is small-ish and new and everything big and old needs to be constantly attacked. That is the one and only law of business. Business is like the Klingon society: you last only as long as you can defend your position, and everyone is always trying to take it all away from you, because everyone wants to be king.

And yeah, in a few years' time, if and when Revolut becomes the new establishment, I'll have something else in my wallet.

I like to support the little guy, but I like to support the little guy that knows how to do business. There was this hair salon in Iași and it went under, and the owner came out with a rant on Facebook about how the city was not ready for her new and innovative hairstyles. I didn't quite get the finer points of the rant, but I got that she was blaming the customer, and that is myopic and entitled and I can't support something like that. Start a small coffee shop and I'll buy your coffee, if it's good. Tell me that I have a moral duty to buy from you, simply because you're small and local, and that means you're lazy and arrogant, and I'll stop being your customer.

Nobody owes you anything and that is true in most places but doubly so in business.

Am I saying that other ways of investing your energies, such as non profits or activism are less worthy? No, I'm not saying that, I don't decide worth and I don't believe in a universal hierarchy of worth. You decide if it's worthy for you and I'm not ever going to judge anyone for choosing what to do with their life. Two of the people I respect most, in the world really, are two ladies from here, from Iași, involved in animal welfare. They are determined, fearless, passionate and, above all, effective. They collaborate with the municipal pound, one of them built a private shelter, they work with and mobilize networks of volunteers and they get a lot done, spending their own money, their own time and their own emotional reserves dealing, sometimes on a moment's notice, sometimes in the middle of the night, with difficult and occasionally horrific cases of animals in dire need of help. They, and the many others with them and around them are, truly, my heroes. Coincidentally or not, these two ladies are also business people. One of them is a small to medium scale real estate developer and the other is, from what I gather, the owner, or general manager, of a small publishing house and printing press. I've only met the former, once. Is it that their business experience has taught them to be effective, or is it that their personality was such that they were going to be effective and proactive no matter what they did, be it helping stray dogs or building houses? I don't know, can't really know for sure, but if they're like most other people, it's probably a mixture of both, a virtuous circle of potential leading to achievement and experience, then further enhancing potential. What's clear is that the, relatively modest but real resources they have, from their businesses, allow them to be more effective in protecting and helping animals than they would otherwise be.

So no, I'm not saying that business is the be all end all of the ways in which you can spend your productive time. I don't own a t-shirt with "capitalism" written on it, although I saw one just the other day and for a second considered it, but I do have to say, and emphasize, that businesses, in a functioning, competitive free market, has a way of forcing the bullshit out, of staying true, of staying useful, that, generally, with few exceptions, you don't find in public administration and you don't find in the nonprofit world.

There's this bar/vegetarian bistro here in Iași, that I actually like as a place, has a nice vibe about it, that's a bit of a hub for the eco/socialist/marxist crowd. I'm not lumping all these together and I'm not saying that they tend go hand in hand, I for example consider myself very eco but definitely not a socialist and no way in hell a marxist. I'm talking about the place and the vibe it sends. A small shop to the left of the bar offers locally produced wallets and handbags and what not made out of recycled billboards. Vintage French newspapers pinned on the walls writing about how *"le capitalisme"* ruined something, probably the sensitive French soul. Water is served only in glass, there is no plastic being used anywhere. If you want, they let you to bring your own spoon, so they use less water to wash theirs. Some of the crowd in places like these is made up of usually smart, suitably blasé, occasionally nihilistic young boys and girls, eager to talk to you about the most sweeping ideas imaginable, the fate of the world, the nature of existence, the evilness of money, all while sipping on their latte. They call themselves activists and some of them spend all their time arguing on forums, before coming back to their latte. I have little patience for this crowd and I would rather engage in a conversation with the owner of this place, a dynamic, action oriented, driven lady that has managed to make this joint, and other things, happen, has created jobs and opportunities in the process, has left and is leaving a mark that is significantly more than snobby comments.

I told you, I like the little guy, but I like the little working guy, not the little complaining guy. You don't like big oil? Me neither. You're that passionate about it? Go put them out of business. Be the next Elon Musk, invent a new battery, do something, don't be the millionth hipster whining about the military-industrial complex.

What I'm trying to say is that, when you have access to a free market, business is, in my opinion, generally the most effective way to invest your time in order to get some kind of concrete, real outcome. I'm not saying it's morally superior, or better in some other way, I'm saying it's geared towards effectiveness in a way that's pretty unique to it. It's no accident that Melinda and Bill Gates want to run their philanthropy foundation, the largest of its kind in the world, with 38 billion dollars in assets, more like a business.

I am pitching to you entrepreneurship and professional excellence as a good life choice.

Now, the big problem with business, especially with big business, is that it's gotten so bureaucratic, so formalized, so directionless that it's hard, for too many people, in too many organizations, to find the kind of personal agency, professional pride and purpose that I'm so bent on having. Part of the onus is on us, on each us, and it's the largest part. We alone are responsible for forging our own path, no one else is, not the boss, not the company, not the government, not anyone but us. I'm trying to teach you how to do just that, because I believe the big problem is chronic and widespread failure of leadership, and the cure is personal responsibility and, unavoidably, leadership.

When I speak about a business career as a philosophical choice, I speak from experience. I've been the latte sipping complainer, though not for very long indeed. I've been the nihilist. I've been defeated. I've been despondent. I'm not some kind of tie wearing manager coming straight out of business school, some kind of teacher's pet. I've been lost, I've been stoned, I've been drunk, I've been absurd, I've been cruel, I've been kind, I've been everything and I want to shake the establishment just as much as the next guy, but I know I'm not going to shake much of anything by simply complaining about it. For myself, I've consciously and with eyes wide open chosen business as the best possible avenue for a life well lived, for the foreseeable future, and for the past 20-ish years of my life.

Ideological leadership

You know what some old communists and some young ones too say, right? They say that communism is a great idea, but it was never applied well in practice, and that's why it failed, so maybe we should try again and see if we have better luck next time.

More managers and leaders than you'd like to think lead in the same way: ideologically. Some have it in their heads that people are lazy and you need to lead with an iron hand, or nothing happens, and then that's how they act, all the time, every time. Some think that all people need is the freedom to be themselves, so they lead by stepping all the way back until they fade into the background. Both styles are self-fulfilling prophecies. The strict manager will never get to see how autonomy and initiative look like under his firm rule because that's not the kind of place where autonomy manifests itself. The abdicating manager will never get to see that some clear direction can sometimes do wonders because he'll never try it. These ideologists, and many others like them, will keep doing the same thing and getting the same results, again and again, curiosity muted, learning stifled. Ideology takes a multitude of forms. Some others worship at the altar of management by objectives, some drool over KPI's and some dream about holacracy. There is no shortage of ideology.

Ideological leadership is when we are so in love with an idea of how we think something should be, that we become unable to clearly see the reality in front of us.

The world is not as we'd like it, the world is how it is. We can try to change it, and indeed we should, but we should start from an accurate representation of the current state. When we are given a situation, a team, some people, it would serve us well to take a good honest look at what we have in front of us. Maybe it so happens that this team is a full of motivated, senior and competent people and indeed, they need little more than to be left alone. Maybe it's a mess of a team, disengaged, plagued by infighting, with a bully terrorizing the juniors and unable to communicate among themselves and, in this case, just letting them be and creating a safe space for them might not be the wisest thing one can do. Whatever it is, recognize it and act appropriately. Don't ideologically apply the same techniques for all situations.

Managers that think they know the answer before they even land and see the situation on the ground may get away with it for a while, but not for long. Ideological leadership is a form of leadership ignorance.

Tony Hsieh, CEO of Zappos, decided that his company should adopt holacracy, a radical system of self-organization and flatness, with no management and no job titles. In 2015 he announced that he was going to do it and he informed his entire company, saying that they would be moving to holacracy and that, among other things, all management roles would go away, and all managers had a few months to find new roles inside the company, or would have to leave. How were they going to find new roles? There was no official HR process or anything centralized, they would have to individually get close to teams and find or create a place for themselves. In the end, 18% of the workforce ended up leaving the company as part of the transition. Many others felt confused, stressed and unsure about what to do. Many liked the new freedom but felt a penalty on productivity. Some relished the new reality in all its aspects. At the time of writing this, the transition is complete, Zappos is still here, Tony is still CEO, and for the first time in eight years, it fell off Fortune's 100 Best Companies to Work For list.

The question is, was Tony and ideological fool to do this? It depends. If he knew what he was doing, he had a vision, and he knew that some people would disagree with it and it would be hard and come with a cost, but he still did it, then he was not an ideological fool. He may have made other mistakes, you may still disagree with him, but I don't consider him a ideological fool. If on the other hand he simply fell in love with holacracy, and that blinded him, made him unable to see reality as it was, he just couldn't stop himself from doing it, because he had to, because he felt compelled to, and that prevented him from even understanding the potential impact or the magnitude of the change then yes, he was an ideological fool.

For the avoidance of confusion, ideological leadership has nothing to do with, for example, the company mission. An overly ambitious or even "absurd" mission, such as wanting to build a rocket and go to Mars with it does not imply ideological leadership. The company mission can be as ideological or as far reaching as you want to have it. The company values also are, by definition, ideological. If you want to behave morally for example, that is of course intransigent and non-negotiable.

Ideological leadership is not about having an ambitious vision, being a radical visionary, or wanting to leave a big legacy behind. Having all these doesn't make you an ideological leader. You are an ideological leader when you are so captivated by a particular idea of how the world should be that you are unable to clearly see the world as it is and you are, therefore, disconnected from reality.

The (still) big ideological divide in leadership at the moment, and for some decades now, has been the big switch from centralized to self organized. From management authority to autonomy. From leadership decision to team consensus. It's a transition I personally, to a large degree, welcome, but I also think it's walking on its last legs and a new phase is about to begin, a phase that will not reverse or erase what came before it, but it will change it and it will put it under a new light. Rooted in the cultural revolution of the 60s, the big arc from a company like the General Motors of the 50's, with its military like structure, to something like today's nearly perfectly decentralized Zappos, has mostly mirrored and followed the social and cultural evolution of western societies as a whole, and it's no surprise that the management ethos of the day is a reflection of the overall cultural ethos of the society in which that management exists. The cultural revolution of the 60s is however done and dead, it just doesn't know it yet. Its massive impact has been realized and its force spent and it's now in its last decadent years, feeding on its own ideas of yesteryear, left with nothing to do but rearrange in new ways what was once fresh and vibrant. Like the French aristocracy of the 18th century, all the current management establishment can do is eat and drink while the going is good. Take a look at the complacency fest that is TED, in as far as the topic of leadership is concerned at least, one of the biggest stages of the management establishment, and you will see how ideologically aligned people come together to applaud on hearing a slightly different version of something they heard an hour before. It's a predictable spectacle, with no ferocity of ideas, with no real challenge to the dominant ideology. What is today's dominant management ideology? It's a weird mixture of one hand empowerment, but on the other hand not getting too involved in a deep, obsessive way, or any other way that is perceived as unhealthy or which goes against the "work life balance" cult. People are alternatively considered very weak and fragile and need all kind of help and safe spaces to be themselves, but then again, it is said that anyone can be anything, and all they have to do is want it and, sometimes, maybe work for it. You're supposed to challenge ideas, but only some ideas, because some are too sacred to question. It's mess, a house of cards ready to fall.

It's ridiculous that we still act like the main problem in leadership today is the authoritarian leader and the good fight is the fight for freedom. That was indeed the fight, and freedom is always worth fighting for, but that's the last war. The big issue now is different and it's one of not enough leadership, of frightened managers, of the diluted responsibility of CEO's, of the averaging and compromising forces of social conformity, of the advancing culture of victimhood and entitlement. We don't need less leadership, we need more, and we don't need less leadership authority, we need more, and we need more guts. Courage is what we're lacking more than anything else, not autonomy. Determination, dedication, a moral code, a path worth following and a vision that's more than PR word soup, that's the leadership we need. Sure, not in the outdated ways of decades gone, and when I say authority in no way do I mean the kind of authority that is simply accepted, in no way am I advocating for obedience, I abhor obedience. I want debate, I want conflict, I want everyone to speak up, but I also want leaders, and everyone, but it starts with the leaders, to feel like they have the authority to make real decisions, to do things that matter, to stop being afraid. Unchecked power corrupts, but the absence of any power paralyzes. We don't need to give less power to our leaders, we need to give them more.

We need purposeful, brave, non-ideological, determined and moral leaders, ready and willing to make decisions that matter, and to go through the hard work and the hard times that will inevitably come, as a matter of general life and cyclical economies, and, in a more private way, for the hardships inevitably awaiting anyone doing anything of real consequence.

Stoic leadership

I love cowboy movies and I think I know why. For one, there's the freedom. The life of a cowboy isn't easy and is full of dangers, but there's no dress code. There's no cocktail party. There's no corporate politics and no finessing of emails so you don't upset some middle manager on the receiving end. The bear may kill you, but you can't blame the bear for trying.

Cowboys are great stoics. "Deserve's got nothing to do with it" said Will Munny, just before shooting and killing Little Bill for torturing and killing his friend. And when Will rode into that town that evening, by himself, straight for Bill, knowing that a dozen or more armed men were already gathered, ready to come looking for him, he did not think about his chances. He did not think about what was fair, or right, or how life should have been different. He did not lament about his situation. He had something to do and he did it, one action at a time. He got on his horse. He rode into town. He went to the saloon. He opened the door. He shot the first guy in his path and then, one by one, he shot the others. It so happened that he won and lived. If he had died at any step along the way, I do not know if he would have felt anything different. He had to do what he had to do, success or failure were, in a way, irrelevant. When you truly really have to do something, you do it. How far you get is inconsequential. You do it with everything you have, with everything you are, and you stop when you're done, or when you're dead. There's no point in talking about it, in how you feel about it, in how you would like it to be.

When Blondie, the man with no name, listens to Tuco's story about how he had been warmly welcomed by his brother, knowing that, in reality, Tuco's brother had just rejected him for the outlaw he was, a disappointment to him and their dead parents, and hears Tuco saying what a good feeling is for even a tramp like him to have a brother somewhere who'll never refuse him a bowl of soup, when in fact he had just been denied that very bowl and that brotherly embrace, Blondie understands Tuco's pain and, knowing he doesn't have to say anything, takes what was left of the cigar he was smoking, lets out a rusty "yeah" and silently hands it to Tuco, who takes it and painfully draws from it as both men ride away with no more words needed. I find this act of kindness and understanding more moving and more relevant than all the coaching in the world. Why is your life the way it is? I do not know my friend. Sure, we can, if we put in the effort, figure out the chain of events that brought you here today, but what will you do with that information? Are you going to wallow in how it could have been, should have been, would have been something else, if only for this or that? Or are you going to get on your horse and start doing what you need to do? Are you going to complain about the unfairness of it all, or are you going to do the act of kindness right in front of you, silently, without feeling the need to tweet about it afterwards? Are you going to stand there looking cool, ready to explain anything away, or are you going to do something?

Stoic leadership is a journey you start and you finish, or you drop trying, not because you're told to, not because society wants you to, not because it's fashionable, but because you choose to.

I had this thing I used to say to my friends when they were complaining about the injustice of the world. I told them that every morning I walk out of my house and someone doesn't shoot in the head and eats my liver, that's another day in which I get to live the miracle of civilization, this beautiful construction of ours where we very rarely eat each other's liver. It's not the natural state of things, nature is a murderous playground. It's something we've built and once you look at it like that, it tends to put things in perspective.

Here is my crash course in stoicism for you: The Good, The Bad and the Ugly, 1966. Unforgiven, 1992. The Seven Samurai, 1954. Marcus Aurelius, Meditations, 180 AD. Fictional cowboys, fictional samurais (strictly speaking samurais were Zen, but Zen and stoicism share half a heart and Kurosawa was an admirer of John Ford so there's other connections here as well), and a real Roman emperor.

The new angels

The possibilities of AI, of life by design, of digitally uploading our brains into the cloud, of enhancing our bodies and minds with cyborg additions, genetic engineering, these are the new limits. We used to look at angels and aspire to get ever closer, knowing we'll never reach. Of course, it's much easier to look up to beings of light than to implants behind your ear. One is perfectly attractive, and one is instinctively repulsive. But then again, one is real and getting realer, and one is not, and not.

I don't know how relevant this book is going to be once these things become reality. I don't know how relevant everything I know or am is going to be once these things start happening. It's a terribly exciting and fascinating kind of fear I feel thinking that I could be, within my lifetime, a witness of the greatest ever transformation of our species, in the shortest imaginable timespan, on the evolutionary scale. Bigger than fire. Bigger than the wheel. Bigger than anything.

But that would be another book and I can't write them both at the same time. I can't write about reality today while second guessing myself at every step. That would be a useless undertaking, so for now I'm writing this book, for us, for homo sapiens. In 20 years, if I write something else, I may have to start but saying that everything in here is obsolete. Or maybe not. For the time being, this is us, this is our world, and we need to lead.

The Fun & Fearless System of Leadership

This is where we start laying out the actual Fun & Fearless Leadership system, a system of effective leadership, with seven distinct steps. A detailed, pragmatic, backed by real examples description of how to start from the beginning and take it all the way, for yourself, for your team or for your company.

Who is the system for?

The Fun & Fearless Leadership System is a set of leadership practices that I've developed based on my experience in software, as a developer, manager, consultant and entrepreneur. There is nothing in it that is specific to software or IT, no specialized terminology, no obstacles against it being applied in other industries, but I have developed it with the flexibility, complexity and decentralization specific to this industry in mind. I expect it to work best in creative work, talent driven projects that have to deal with ambiguity, discovery, adaptation and innovation.

The system is designed from the ground up for the new generations of leaders and talent, who care about the *why*, who look for meaning, who have expectations of fast, relevant and exciting experiences, and who have no implicit loyalty to a company just because that's what society expects of them. They will not wade through the corporate drudgery for years on end just because that's what they're told to do. They need to be continuously "sold" the job, a paycheck will simply not be enough for them to give their best. They also care about the company's reputation, about its values, and the personal moral and professional standing of the leaders of that company. They will avoid the companies they perceive not to be worthy of their ideals.

In terms of size, I've considered anything from individual consultants, startups, small and medium size companies and up to corporations. I truly believe this system applies everywhere, although it has to be said that an excessive amount of bureaucracy, politics and corporate dysfunctionality will affect and suppress leadership behaviors of any kind, not only those recommended by me here. That having been said, the fact is that, even in the worst contexts, you'll be better off with the system rather than without it, and you'll also learn more about how to spot and correctly diagnose a bad culture if nothing else.

In terms of seniority, it can be adopted by anyone from the aspiring junior team leader to the CEO. Clearly, the CEO will use it for more consequential decisions, but as with any good leadership behaviors, it's never too soon to start and it's not tied to hierarchy. Some techniques will come easier to people that also have a formal authority because they can simply decide what less senior employees can only influence, but fundamentally this is a system about your own behaviors and your relationships with others, regardless of your position in the hierarchy. It is not a system of formal power and formal decision making, it is a system of, first and foremost, personal leadership.

As far as the technical knowledge you need to properly understand this book and the system, there's not really any. The concepts are explained in plain English, using as simple of a vocabulary as possible. There's nothing in here about the "technical" part of management, because this is not a book about management: we won't talk about budgets, forecasts, Gantt charts or anything of that sort. We will discuss how you listen, talk, make decisions, communicate, engage with people and while these concepts have non-trivial sophistication behind them, they can be described using everyday language. A basic understanding of psychology and sociology is the most useful type of outside knowledge you can bring, but don't abandon if you don't have it, I'll give you enough context to properly understand the system even without it. I want to say though that an appreciation for the human mind and human nature is going to be required of you as a leader, generally speaking, but if this is the first book to open that world to you, you will still be able to successfully read and understand it.

Culturally, my system relies on personal ownership, clear and direct communication and a readiness to engage in constructive conflict. If this worries you a little, it's normal, most of us feel that way when we first think about it. It's a perfectly natural homo sapiens reaction to want to avoid conflict. I'll walk you through it step by step and don't worry, the Fun & Fearless system is not a battle technique, it's a system of compassionate, moral and respectful leadership, but I do highlight the need for the occasional uncompromising position and for very direct feedback.

Lastly, my system is not for everyone. It could be for everyone, in as any intelligent person could apply it, but it's an active system, it requires motivation and intentional action, it's a system of involved, present leadership. Do not adopt this system if you're not ready to engage in deliberate leadership, aiming for impact. Not for one second should that be confused with micromanagement or overbearing control, far from it, the opposite actually, but it does require the will and desire to take your leadership seriously, constantly make decisions and then own them unwaveringly.

The system is laid out as a series of 7 Steps, each having several Leadership Techniques grouped under it, with anecdotes, examples and bits of relevant theory. Everything is meant to challenge you, put you on the spot, and potentially cause you discomfort. There is no growth without discomfort. Discomfort is not misery, discomfort is the edgy cousin of exhilaration, and I'll teach you how to love it.

If your goal is to explicitly adopt the system in a team or a company than you should do it methodically, in order, and understand that some steps won't work at all without the previous ones. If however you're just looking read a good book and are curious to jump ahead and read some chapter down the line, feel free to do that. Most other steps refer back to "Step 1 – A long, hard look in the mirror "and "Step 3 – The Miracle of Compassionate Radical Honesty" so you may want to start with these, but other than this, any reading order will work.

I will give many examples from my work and experience. All the stories and tell in here are real and they have happened as laid out in this book. I will, however, anonymize and change identifying details, without altering the core of the situation. A he may become a she or vice versa. I may change company details. I may change a nationality, or I may make other changes to ensure anonymity, while at the same time leaving the story intact enough to keep its meaning.

Throughout the book, I will frequently say that the leader must do this or that, and that it is her responsibility to make sure that certain things happen. I do not mean to imply that the rest of the team is passive, complacent and waiting for the leader to do or say everything. Far from it, I strongly believe in empowered, active and proactive teams. At the end of the day, however, the leader is accountable that the things that need to happen, happen. Does she do them herself, does she need to only say the word and delegate, or is the team so autonomous and empowered that things happen without her intervention? Whichever way it may be, she must make sure the right things happen, and this one thing can not be delegated. You can not delegate final responsibility, that is why it's called final. So when I say that the leader must do this or that, it is a simplified way of saying that she must make sure those things happen. Her style of making it happen is another question.

It's hard, but you can do it

Before you continue, allow me to discourage you. Don't take my words of discouragement lightly: there's no shame if you change your mind. There are real, valid reasons why you might want to turn around.

Sure, there's no downside in educating yourself with some leadership skills, on top of your core job, but if we're talking about actual, formal leadership responsibilities, impacting projects, budgets and most of all, people, that needs to be taken seriously. Leadership is serious stuff and there's leadership failure everywhere you look. Companies fail miserably, cultures go rotten, laws are broken, jobs are lost, people are hurt, the environment is destroyed, all due to failure of leadership. We don't need more of this. This is not a game for the weak. I'm personally invested in you being a solid, strong and moral leader because we share, if nothing else, a planet.

As a leader with formal accountability for a team, you will spend your days doing more work, with more responsibility, taking more worries home with you, sleeping worse at night than pretty much any other member of your team. You will work really hard to motivate and organize people that may or may not be as good or as dedicated as you were when you were in their place. People's behaviors can be the best kind of reward, and they can be the worst kind of disappointment. Prepare for both.

Starting down this path also means that you will, not right away but in a few years for sure, lose your technical skills. You used to be a great developer say, but not anymore, you are now a manager. It may not be such a good trade as you initially thought. I typically advise against one particular kind of manager, the dedicated people manager. Be a manager if you want to, but keep delivering something, keep building something, run projects, own products and yes, indeed, lead and manage people to that end, but don't turn into some kind of a glorified HR, doing nothing all day but hearing people's gripes and organizing their performance evaluations. That should not be your main activity. Your main activity, as a manager, should be delivering something and yes, also building and leading a great team for that purpose.

The business world has too many so-called leaders that got into it because they wanted to feel more important than the guy at the next desk, or thought that they'd get a few extra bucks, or saw an inspirational YouTube clip and thought to themselves that must be it, or for a million other wrong reasons and now they're unhappy and stuck or, worse, happily ignorant, unaware of their own flaws, messing everybody else's business.

Don't be one of them. This book is about not being one of them.

If you just want to add some leadership skills to your core job, do it. The work of the future, hell, the work of today, demands this of you. Leadership is not just for formal leaders anymore and hasn't been for a while. We all need to be leaders if we're to be successful, no matter what we do. It's just how it is.

And if you really want to be a leader, go all in, become a manager, start a company, make this leading thing your primary concern, then this is the book for you. It's not going to be easy, but nothing worthwhile is.

Step 1: A long, hard look in the mirror

Scorpions and marshmallows

There's the old fable of the frog and the scorpion, and it goes like this.

One evening, the scorpion approaches the pond and tells the frog sitting there at the edge of water:
"*Frog, will you let me stand on your back while you cross the pond, so I may get to the other side without drowning?*"
"*Scorpion,*" replies the frog, "*I would, I really would, but I am afraid you will sting me and I will die, because you are a scorpion*"
"*Frog, but I have no interest in stinging you and no reason to even consider it. Think, if I were to sting you while you're carrying me across the water, I would sink and die as well, as I can not swim. Why would I do that?*", argues the scorpion
Uneasy still about the prospect of having a scorpion on its back, but convinced by the logic of its arguments, the frog agrees, and they start crossing the pond, scorpion on the back of the frog. They barely make it to the middle when the scorpion stings and mortally poisons the frog. Sinking, the frog mutters:
"*But why, treacherous scorpion, why? Now we shall both die!*"
"*Blame me not*", replies the scorpion, accepting its fate: "*It is not me, it is my nature*".

It's a beautiful story that speaks not only about the power of our nature but also about the irrationality of our behaviors. We understand what we should logically do and yet we frequently choose to act against our self-interest because we are compelled by our "nature". The argumentative person will argue, even when they logically know they should be more accepting of other people's ideas. They will regret it every time, as soon as they're out of the room, as soon as they open their mouth, and then they will do it again the next day. The over critical boss will have heard about the virtues of encouraging his people more but will snap into the comfortable pattern of sharply criticizing them for every little mistake. We are trapped in our own tendencies and engage in regrettable action, even when we have a superior rational understanding of a better way. We fight our nature for a while, but if we're unable to change it or at least feel like we're making sufficient progress, most of us give up and just accept it, saying to ourselves, *"that's just who I am."*

The philosophical idea behind the frog and scorpion story is that of a deep and profound fixed identity, of that which we are and which we can sometimes control, but, when put under pressure, always comes back to dictate our behavior. The unchanging part, that which we are and which we can never truly alter.

Contradicting this, modern research has, to a large degree, downplayed the idea of nature and focused on context, that is, the idea that people's behaviors are driven more by the situation they're in at any given time rather than some deep hardwired unchanging personality. When you're very hungry you are more likely to lie to get food than when you have a full belly. In a meeting, if those around have already supported an opinion, you are less likely to have the opposite view than if you had been the first to speak. Even the famous marshmallow test has been recently revisited. A seminal 60's study of delayed gratification, kids were offered one marshmallow now or two marshmallows in 15 minutes. The researchers wrote down which kid chose what and then tracked those kids throughout life and saw that the ones that waited for 15 minutes grew up to have better school grades, better health, better careers and so on. The obvious conclusion, it seemed, was that delayed gratification was very important to success and, furthermore, it was a trait observable as early as childhood. More recently, another team redid the experiment, with more kids, and found a different correlation, specifically that children coming from more affluent families found it easier to wait for 15 minutes, the idea being that those kids had learned at home that they regularly tended to get things and so they didn't feel the need to rush and grab what was in front of them right away. They had the luxury of patience. Poor kids, on the other hand, had learned to take what they could, when they could, uncertain about when the next meal would come. Behavior driven not by the kid's nature, but by the kid's circumstances. And if we will trace these new batch of kids throughout their lives, we might very well find that those who waited for 15 minutes will have more success than those that didn't, but will it be because they knew how to delay the gratification of a marshmallow, or will it be because they came from affluent families, and that will help them in so many other ways on their path to success?

The interplay of nature and context is going to be a theme throughout this book. I will require of you the sophisticated understanding of context, but I will also ask for the unwavering accountability that comes when true leaders commit, regardless of context and how it may change and influence you.

Are leaders born or made? Is it in their nature, is it in their context, is it learned?

I do not know the answer to this question. Or, better said, I know a lot of answers to this question, but there is no "42" at the end of it, no one definitive conclusion, no single prediction you can make. I know you can learn and grow in remarkable and unexpected ways, I've seen it. I know it's very hard to learn and grow in some other ways, and some challenges are damn near impossible, I've seen that too.

In the absence of objective clarity, I've made a decision that best suits my utilitarian needs: this is not the right question. There are two other, better questions. The first is, what should a leader do about herself and about her people? Should she focus on existing natural strengths only and hone those, or should she aim to develop new, unnatural skills as well? The answer to this question is a resounding "it depends" and we'll be discussing specific situations throughout the book. It depends on the person in question, on team size, on the nature of the problem, on the specific situation. There is a time and a place to bunker down and double down on your strengths and there is a time and a place to explore new dimensions of personal development.

The second questions is even trickier. When it comes to context, should she attribute behaviors and results to context, or to individual willpower and effort? I can not overemphasize the importance of answering this right and, while on some level the answer is also "it depends", there is a general way to look at it and the way you look at this is key to your understanding of leadership. On one hand, leaders that attribute everything to individual will are very blunt instruments indeed. They judge on results alone. You did it or you didn't do it, don't tell me about context, I don't want to hear it. These leaders will aim to teach the hungry kid to not reach for the marshmallow rather than feed the kid and satiate his burning need to get the snack. But then again, they may actually manage to do it. This kind of leaders are all about individual responsibility and accountability and they strongly believe in willpower. On the other hand, leaders that attribute most behaviors to context will have a nuanced understanding of situations and will strategically change environments to influence behavior in smart ways, but they will be bad at demanding any kind of real personal responsibility, because they fundamentally don't believe in it. While in some way they may be more right, that is, have a better understanding of human nature looked at it in a scientific way, leaders that focus too much on context will have a very difficult time creating a culture of action, a culture of getting things done. Philosophical analysis of nuances is not usually a recipe for success in business, particularly not when it stops you from asking clear things from those around you, and from yourself.

What if your answer is both? It's not a good answer. Yes, you know that both context and willpower matter and on some level you do account for both, but your bias, your tendency, your attitude, your behavior, your example and the culture you want to create, they will have to lean one way or the other. You have to choose, and any choice is better than no choice. That is why the true question is what do you want to believe? Yes, you read that right. What do you *want* to believe? Context matters, will matters, sometimes one breaks the other, sometimes it's the other way around but the crucial thing, the only thing that matters, is what kind of example do you want to set and what kind of culture do you want to have, and that is your decision to make and you must make it. Do you want a culture of accountability or do you want a culture of nuanced contextual sophistication? My choice is clear and it is, always, to have a bias for personal accountability. I understand context, I work with context and I teach my people to understand it and work it but, at the end of the day, when you ask me who is responsible for something or another, I will say John, or Mary, but it will be one name and one name only. I will not say "John, but only if the context is favorable". I will not say "Mary, but only if she's lucky". I will give you one name. And when you ask me who's responsible for everything, as the leader, I will say that I am. And that will be the end of that conversation.

If you want to have a conversation about society as a whole, history, the broad strokes of human evolution, then we'll discuss the incredible importance of context. A population with access to education and modern medicine will be vastly different than the same population without access to these things, even though their nature as human beings and individuals is the same. At sufficiently large scales, for long periods of time, statistically speaking, context is king. If you want to discuss the history of business, we will again dedicate ample room to context, we will discuss the industry changing innovations and the different stages of the industrial revolution. If, however, you want to get something done now, with those few people over there you call your team, then we need to start talking about individual accountability and we need to name names. If you want me to think about the long term growth of the company, I will consider such statistical probabilities as the kind of people we're hiring, their education, prior experience, onboarding processes and the overall culture and systems we'll need to have in place. In a word, I will think about context and how I can shape it. If you want to talk about this product that we need to get out this year, I will again need to start talking about names and what each of those names is accountable for.

As a leader, your job is to deliver effective leadership. It has to work. You have to see yourself as able to influence the situations you're in, you can't sit back and blame context and be blasé about it. You have to be able to make your people feel the same way, that their actions matter and they can fight terrible odds and win, whatever the context. Like general Patton said, *"Our basic plan of operation is to advance and to keep on advancing regardless of whether we have to go over, under, or through"*. Your culture has to be one of action, of individual responsibility and of personal agency. What you do matters. What everyone does, and doesn't do, matters.

What about luck? Luck is great and you should want more of it. By definition, you can't control it. You can sometimes take a variable out of the luck (uncontrolled, unpredictable) area and move it into the business parameter area, make it something you can control. When it comes to actual luck however, what you can do is identify and maximize luck generating behaviors. Where does luck happen in your business? Does luck come with people? Then go meet more people. Does luck come in the form of sudden consumer excitement about your great product? Then try more marketing.

Let's say luck is when a flying bird shits on you. You can't control birds, so you can't directly control luck, but there are some things you can control. For one, luck is never going to hit if you stay indoors. Once outside, there's more luck in the park under the trees than on the side of the street. There's more luck in summer than in winter. So be more in parks, on summer days, and you might get lucky. That's how luck works. Understand it, maximize it, no point complaining about it.

What's your cheetah skill?

The cheetah is the fastest land animal in the world, having been observed to run at speeds of up to 112km/h. The second fastest is the Springbok Antelope, clocked in at up to 88km/h. Cheetahs frequently hunt springboks. Seeing a cheetah in action is a thing of wonder. Thin and light, it has enlarged nostrils to get all the oxygen it needs to run at that speed, pushing air into its lungs, not unlike a jet engine. Its huge tail is expertly used for extremely sharp, unreal looking turns, and their claws, unlike most felines, are semi-retractable only, providing better grip in the savannah dirt. A series of other major and minor evolutions, from their bones and joints to how they move, have made them the perfect running machine.

The cheetah is the best in the world at running really really fast, second to none. That's why cheetahs can hunt and catch prey that other predators, such as lions, don't even bother having a try at.

And yet, the cheetah can run at this pace for maybe a couple of minutes, if that. After a successful kill, she will drag her prey to a shaded place and then spend up to an hour panting, collecting her breath, exhausted, unable to do much of anything else, not strong enough to even take a bite out of the animal she just caught and killed. In those few minutes of sheer brilliance, she gave it all. If a single hyena happens to stumble upon the cheetah during this time, our lighting fast hunter will have no choice but to abandon the kill. The very same adaptations that make cheetahs the best speed runners, light body, thin elegant bones, also make them very poor fighters, so they don't even try. Never mind that they might easily get killed if they stood their ground, any kind of injury that might prevent them from running at full speed would mean almost certain death by starvation.

What is your cheetah skill? What are you really good at and what comes as naturally to you as running to the cheetah? And once you find it, should you just keep doing that one thing, or should you at some point put some real effort into developing some new skills as well?

I once worked with a manager that was brilliant at interpersonal skills, at improvising solutions, at fixing emotional situations, getting the best out of conflicts and somehow turning fuckups into positives that could reenergize and refocus teams. He was not only very good at it, he was a natural, he loved it, he felt great doing it. Nothing put a smile on his face like being handed a hot mess of a situation and being told he had to fix it in a hurry, as long as the situation did not involve much planning or any bureaucracy. The flipside was that he had no real reason to develop complementary skills, like planning and avoidance of crisis situations. His hammer was fixing problems quickly and every situation he saw was a candidate for his favorite medicine: go in, sort things out, motivate, negotiate, get it done. While praising him for this, I also tried to get him to open up to a more strategic way of management, be more of a planner, avoid problems rather than simply revel in fixing them, learn how to prioritize, understand that not everything should be allowed to turn into a fire that needs fighting. He tried, for my sake, but was reluctant and did it without gusto. Worse, the strain of fighting with himself and his own tendencies sapped his enthusiasm and soon enough he started losing effectiveness overall. It wasn't only difficult to add a new skill, but the process was weakening his existing skills, like some kind of strong medicine that was attacking his immune system. I was making things worse. I was making him worse, or at least it seemed that way. Was I, without realizing, trying to teach a cheetah how to swim and in the process asking him to run slower, messing with his primary drive? Yes, I was and It's not necessarily wrong to try, but I was wrong to do it without understanding what I was doing and also, I was, to a degree, doing it for the wrong reasons. I was attached to an idea of a "complete manager" and I was trying to make everyone get close to it. That was a mistake. I wasn't wrong to tell him that he needed better planning to move to the next level, that was true and needed saying, but the way in which I did it was naive. I expected him to do it easily and with the same dedication as he was doing the things he loved doing, and that was not going to happen.

There are two ways to learn. The first kind is to get better at that which you already love. The cheetah learns how to run faster, take a tighter turn, last longer. This is investing in your strength and is almost always a good idea. We don't do enough of it and far too often we waste our potential for brilliance by trying to minimize our weaknesses instead of increasing our strengths, as we try to become these well behaved, well rounded pupils, amazing at nothing, pretty good at several things, decent at most. What a waste!

My personal cheetah skill is associative and intuitive thinking: I'm very good at absorbing information just by glancing at it, from many sources, many fields, and then somehow putting it together in a way that more often than not makes sense, and I get to that sense faster than most. I can conceptualize complex situations, even when I only have incomplete and disparate information. I constantly hone my cheetah skill and I try to put myself in contexts where I can best use it. That's why I don't like procedural, process oriented companies for example, because I get bored and the sequentiality and formality they demand pretty much nullify my cheetah skill. In that kind of an environment, I am underutilized, counter-utilized. I thrive in ambiguity, I wither away in bureaucracy. I know that about myself.

The second kind of learning is unnatural, it's teaching the cheetah how to swim, and, more importantly, how to love the water. It's an expensive and risky investment, but a new you can emerge out of this fiery forge of learning something so completely different, and at the end of this long and tortuous road there is the potential for a kind of exponential development, a breakthrough that separates the merely very good leaders from the extraordinary. It is the ultimate way to step out of your comfort zone. There's no guarantee that it will make you great, but I've rarely seen anyone great without it.

When, back in my early years, I had to present a technical idea to a handful of colleagues, in a meeting room in our office, I could barely sleep for three days in terrified anticipation and to this day I don't remember what I told them. When, soon after that, I had to make a case, also on a technical issue, to 20 or 30 developers, colleagues of mine, I again didn't sleep the night before, felt like puking all that morning and, when the moment came, froze after hello. All I could do was drop my pen, on purpose, under the table, so I could gain a few seconds looking for it. I don't remember anything else from that meeting. Faced with these experiences, I had a choice to make. I could stick to what I was good at and carve a successful career that avoided these very uncomfortable public speaking type of situations, and I knew very well I could that, such a career was possible, at hand, and potentially very rewarding. I could just be a cheetah and run free for the rest of my life, not worrying about anything else. Or, alternatively, I could dive into the deep end, face my fears and start the long and unnatural road of learning how to swim. I chose the latter and, in the following years, I invested hundreds of hours into facing my fear, by seeking and exposing myself to the most uncomfortable situations I could find, by preparing, studying and, basically, just doing it, again and again, until it no longer felt horrible but only very bad, and then kind of bad, and then it got easier, until it felt better, until it felt good, until it felt great. Was the investment worth it? On some narrow level, no, I don't make a living by speaking at conferences but, on a deeper level, yes, oh yes, it was so worth it. By facing such a weakness, by conquering such a fear, by going through this long and arduous process, I learned so much more than how to comfortably speak to groups of people without freezing in terror. I learned about me, I learned about others and I learned about what I can do with the right kind of motivation and determination. I gained exponentially more than the ability to stand up on a stage and convey a point. It was a massive effort and it's not the kind of learning you can do all the time, and some people won't even do it once in their whole lives. To you, I recommend it, and I suggest you ask it of your best people. Find your own tortuous road of self-improvement and start that most difficult of all journeys. Change your shape, face your fears. Become something more. And then do it again, at least one major transformation a year. Don's stop. When you stop, you die.

When I tried to tell my manager from above to love planning, I was asking him to do the very unnatural thing of the cheetah learning how to swim. That's fine, but the problem was I didn't know what I was really asking him to do. I thought it was routine, but it wasn't. The way I should have done was to know if I just wanted him to learn some quick, tactical planning or, if I wanted him to truly internalize it, go through this unnatural, transformative learning and, if that's what I wanted, then communicate that clearly, empathetically, convey the magnitude and complexity and what I was asking him to do and then offer the support he needed.

Develop your Mental Sherlock

Introspection is the examination of your own thoughts and feelings. Introspection is something that everyone does but the good leader needs to do it all the time, and better than most. In my experience, one of the biggest predictors for leadership success is one's ability to stop and think about what you're doing and why, understand the chain of thoughts that got you there, be able to unpack your experiences and opinions by detaching yourself from your own emotions and thoughts and analyzing them as if they were someone else's. This is a hallmark of people that manage to learn radically new ideas and truly, dramatically increase their performance. For this to be possible, a lot of things need to happen.

First, you need a good vocabulary for thoughts and feelings. It's very difficult to understand why you're feeling in a certain way if you can't even name that feeling. People that are not used to thinking about their own mind find it very strange the first time they start doing it. It's like the difference between a regular person being in love, feeling it deeply but only able to verbalize it as "gosh, I love you so much", and a poet, who can describe love with such expression and precision that it will be familiar and insightful to anyone that has ever loved. You need to be a poet of your own mind.

Our mind has a rational part, which is the you that are reading this right now, and an older, subconscious, more instinctive part, that's maybe making you feel in a certain way as you read it. Let's call this part Bob. Bob is something, not quite a person, but some being of some sort. He can't speak, but he feels, has motivations, wants to do things and how we treat him determines how he treats us. Bob is our instincts and he and our rational reasoning are more interdependent than we'd like to think. In most decisions, we usually end up doing what Bob wants and then we come up with a rational explanation for why, a process called rationalization, and we then believe our own rationalizations, although they're frequently fake news. You will tell me that you bought a car because you carefully examined its features, but, more often than not, that's only how you convinced your rationality to agree to a decision Bob had already made. Bob already knew what car he wanted when he saw it, you just needed an excuse to agree with him and to make your rational mind feel like it's in charge. It wasn't the spreadsheet with pros and cons that determined which car you bought, it was Bob.

How do we get a handle on this Bob situation? We sherlock the hell out of everything we think and feel, out of every urge, impulse, apprehension, eagerness, fear and desire we have. We stare at the murky waters of our mind until we understand what every ripple means, what deep movement might have caused it and why. Introspection on steroids.

I was working with a business leader in the form of bi-weekly one to one, one hour meetings, where I helped him work through his business and team issues, both through questions and observation, but also through advise. Soon enough, after just a couple of meetings, I started to get this feeling that there was something that I didn't like in the behavior of this client and that this something, unless fixed, would stop him from being a truly effective leader in his organization. Problem was, I didn't know what that something was. It was a feeling I had, like an aftertaste I was left with after our sessions, but I couldn't really put my finger on it. It wasn't something specific, not something he did or didn't do in a single particular situation we discussed, or in our interaction. And yet, this feeling didn't leave me, it only got stronger each time we met. I had to understand it and address it because if I left alone it had the potential to make me dislike my client and that would have affected my relationship with him, so I proceeded to sherlock it.

First question I asked myself: what exactly was I feeling? After some deep thinking and probing, I realized that what I was feeling was a kind of frustration and an urge to step in and fix the situation right then and there. It was very different from all the other feelings I was feeling during my work with this client, where I was calm, collected and composed in my reflection and advice. This urge however, this itch, was different, compelling, urgent and so I had a first clue, that whatever it was, it was something touching a nerve in me, and that's useful to know, because I have a decent understanding of what usually triggers me. It was a starting point.

Second question I asked myself: what exactly in the client's words and actions was triggering this feeling in me? After recalling our discussions in as much detail as I could and replaying them in the back of my mind, on and off, for a few days, it suddenly hit me: avoidance. I had seen hints and indications of avoidance behavior in the way in which this leader was talking about situations and people. In particular, I had seen hints of avoidance in the way in which he was talking about giving feedback to his own direct reports. It wasn't ever very clear or explicit, but it was there in between the lines. Once I figured this out, I immediately understood why it irked me so much: for me, direct confrontation is a crucially important value and something I look for in all leaders. With 3% on the Agreeableness scale on the Big 5 personality test, I know that I strongly prefer truth over harmony. In fact, what that 3% means is that I am willing to sacrifice emotional comfort, mine or others', for the sake of truth, more than 97% of other people. I am among the 3% most direct individuals from those who ever took that test.

Third question I asked myself: is my feeling justified? Of course it upset *me*, I have a strong preference for directness, but besides my personal bias for confrontation, is the situation objectively deserving of correction? Is the nature and degree of avoidance I'm seeing in him a real impediment to his leadership? After putting aside my own feelings as best I could and considering the situation as dispassionately as possible, I reached the conclusion that yes, it was a real issue and I should give him my feedback on it and explore it further.

Fourth question I asked myself: how can I be sure? Armed with these insights, I went into the next weekly meeting ready to carefully observe this aspect. Not yet ready to give any feedback, I was now looking to see if what I thought I had been seeing was really there. True enough, there it was. Specific, significant examples of clear avoidance behavior were there. I was also mindful of the Confirmation bias in me, which is a cognitive bias where, when we want to find something, we tend to see it even when it's not there. Virgin Mary's face in a potato kind of confirmation bias. To counter it, I took notes during our sessions, in my notepad, of those instances where I saw avoidance behaviors, as verbatim as I could, which I could then reflect on and bring back as examples when I would give him my feedback, in the next session.

Using deliberate introspection I was able to start from a murky nagging feeling and go all the way to clear, actionable, specific feedback I strongly felt held real value for my client and was going to help him significantly.

The easiest way to think about this kind of enhanced introspection is like having a Mental Sherlock in your mind, always observant about what's happening in your mind, paying attention to details, interpreting them, putting two and two together, formulating hypotheses, constantly speaking to you about what's happening in your own head, at all levels, rational and instinctive. People not used with introspection don't distinguish well between their rational and irrational selves, it's all mixed and they find themselves reacting to situations in ways which surprise them too, but still couldn't tell you exactly what happened, why they did what they did, nor are they well equipped to truly learn from what happened. This Mental Sherlock's voice is not Bob's voice, it's still a rational voice, but it's elevated from the ground floor of your thinking and looking outside in on both your rational and your instinctive processes. Just picture Benedict Cumberbatch sitting right there in a corner of your head, dark gray overcoat and hat, constantly observing and pointing out all the relevant developments in your mind, keeping your informed, aware, sharp and honest with yourself. Any other image will do if Benedict is not to your liking. Imagine Siri if you prefer, or anyone you want to, it's entirely your choice.

Develop your own Mental Sherlock and create a habit out of having him, or her, constantly ask you questions such as: Why am I feeling this? Why don't I want to do this, what's the big deal? What am I afraid of? Why do I dislike this person, why do they make me want to leave the room? Why am I so ready to agree to this, what conflict am I trying to avoid? How am I likely to react if they do this? How can I be prepared so I don't lose my cool if they do that? Etc.

Your Mental Sherlock is in effect your internal emotional and cognitive radar. If this sounds weird to you, know it sounded weird to me too, but I got used to it and now I can't live without it and I think you will learn to love it too. The Mental Sherlock is not there to sabotage or scare you, nor is it meant to confuse your thinking for no real gain. He is there to give you confidence and speed in your decisions, and help you better understand yourself. If you're prone to darker thoughts and are afraid he'll make you sad, then create an encouraging, supportive Sherlock. On the other hand, if you're cocky and overconfident, then maybe Sherlock needs to remind you that you're not the center of the universe.

In terms of educating yourself on the mind, the list of useful reading is huge, but start with the list of cognitive biases on Wikipedia. Good art is also great at explaining the human mind. Even if sometimes imprecise or outdated in scientific terms, the great psychological novels for example have a unique way of unpacking what's going on in our heads and making us understand just how complex we are. I read Proust's In Search of Lost Time in my teens and even though most of the 4000 pages were, objectively speaking, repetitive, the way in which he looks into his own mind and into the minds of others, the care and attention he pays to emotions, feelings and thoughts, the experience of reading that was life changing for me because it was the first time when I really understood how complicated we are, as human beings, and it taught me to pay real attention to what's happening in my head. If you're just curious, read the first 30 pages or so, the going to sleep opening scene from Swann's Way; it doesn't get better than that in the other 3970, there's just more of it.

Shorter books work too. Catcher in the Rye is a good one. In Cold Blood. Pulp Fiction is a good movie to watch, the way in which they verbalize and discuss their own states of mind is brilliant. The Netflix series Mindhunter about psychopathic killers will help as well; learning about extreme minds helps you better understand more average minds too.

Learning & unlearning

Your Mental Sherlock is going to help you better react to situations and make decisions, but it's also going to make you capable of much better learning. You will better understand how you absorb new information and develop new habits. You will know how far you can push yourself. It's like you've been driving a car based on engine sound alone and suddenly you're given dashboards.

A particularly difficult kind of learning is unlearning: breaking habits, getting outside of some frame of reference, seeing things in a new way.

I told you, just a few pages back, in my cheetah chapter, about that manager I was working with who was really good at putting fires out but not that good at planning to prevent those fires from happening in the first place. His challenge was not in learning new things, it wasn't like the ideas and techniques of planning overwhelmed him intellectually and he couldn't grasp the point of prevention and the mechanics of a todo list. His real challenge was one of unlearning existing, deeply ingrained, internalized and satisfying behaviors. Every time he tried to do the new things I was asking him to do, to plan, he did it with half a heart, because it was unfamiliar, unsatisfying behavior. Every time he stopped doing that and jumped back into his familiar problem solving routines, he felt great again, dopamine flowed. He was in control, he was in the flow, he understood what was happening, he knew what he had to do, and he did it, with satisfying effectiveness. He was falling back on familiar habits and he was falling back on familiar frames of mind. When looking at a situation, his first intuition was not about how he could foresee and prevent, but about what he could fix and how. That was his frame. Managers are sometimes like art critics: two can look at the exact same painting and come up with radically different interpretations. Two can look at the same team, at the same situation, and see radically different things that need addressing. His hammer was intuitive, on the spot, problem fixing, so he when he looked he saw the current states of mind, he detected tensions, vibes, gripes, and he dived in to make it better. When I looked at it I saw what he saw too, probably not as well, but I did not focus on that part, because I was not interested in solving things on the spot. Instead, I was interested in stable long term relationships, purpose and team operating rules. We looked at the same situation and, with our different frames of interest, we saw different things and had different priorities. Putting our frame aside and seeing with new eyes was not about understanding how, we were both smart enough to get that easily. The hard part was stopping, even for a minute, from thinking in our familiar patterns and looking at the situation with dispassionate, clear eyes. Unlearning.

Just the other day I was talking, separately, to two managers, from the same company, about a situation. One of them had demanded from a third colleague more accountability and better results, and she did it in a pretty direct and forceful way. That third colleague took it hard and was upset about it, feeling he had been treated unfairly. The second manager was this third colleague's manager. Talking to the first manager, the one that asked for more accountability, the entire frame of the story was one of responsibility and expansive ownership. She expected that guy to own an area of the project and just do whatever needed to be done, because that's what people do in her frame of expectations. Recalling the event, she kept talking about getting stuff done, about needing to move forward, about taking initiative, being proactive. My conversation with the other manager, who was that guy's line manager and hadn't been present when the exchange happened and was called in to fix the situation with an upset employee, was as different from the previous one as night and day. His frame was entirely different. He talked about the need to be fair with people, he talked about the fine points of exactly what that person owned and didn't and what was fair to expect of him and what not, and he talked about the complex machinery of delivering a big software project and the interplay of roles and responsibilities. Coincidentally or not, the two managers were also incentivized to think differently: the first was charged with delivering. The second was charged with keeping people happy and performing, and also to keep them in the company. Both of these managers would have no issue intellectually understanding the other's frame of reference, it wasn't like they couldn't get it. It wasn't difficult to get. What was difficult was putting their own frame aside for a moment.

Unlearning is almost always harder than learning but it's almost always, fundamentally, more transformative.

In my late teens, I wanted to be free of all preconceived ideas and all that school and society might have put in my head, I wanted it all out, I wanted to make sure that the ideas in my head were my own. To do this, I developed this metaphor, this image, of a nuclear holocaust and a post-apocalyptic landscape. I imagined my familiar surroundings completely destroyed, nothing left alive, only ruins left standing, and then I imagined things slowly, gradually, coming back. The first new blade of grass, the first new tree. It was a game I played in my head for a year, on and off, and I told myself that I would nuke my mind just like I was imagining that post-apocalyptic world in my head. It was my metaphor for erasing all existing ideas and any new life, any new ideas, would be deliberate, understood, of my creation, my own. It was idealistic, sure, extreme, but it also worked. I kept at it daily, I went to bed thinking about it, I thought about it on the way to school and on the way back. I spent a year and hundreds of hours learning how to unlearn and then to learn again and it was the beginning that was hardest. Once I got comfortable with the emptiness, with that desolate world, and with the idea that I would have to fill it, not with dogma but with wisdom, as much as I could do wisdom, and once that clicked, then it all got better and easier.

You can help people unlearn and see in new frames in many ways. You can gently guide them, with questions, with the Socratic method. You can use different words and concepts and dialogue choices to reframe their own ideas in a new way and subtly, almost subversively, make them see that there's another way to look at things. You can aggressively confront them. You can shock them. The best strategy will depend on the situation and your personalities. The beginning is the hardest. The most difficult thing to grasp is that there is not just one frame of reference, but two. This is the wow moment, the step from one to two. The step from two to ten, or from ten to a thousand, that's easier.

For clarity, I'm not making the case for some extreme relativization of truth. I'm not saying that you should agree that 2 plus 2 is 5, because it's not, but I am saying that many things, when it comes to people and leadership, are not as clear cut as arithmetic and, in those situations, truth is, indeed, a matter of choice. Do you demand extreme accountability and risk losing people or do you protect feelings and risk not delivering? What is true? There is no universally valid equation to answer this. It's a choice you must make and if you are to make it informed, you should understand, at the very least, your own frame of reference, if not the others' frame of reference. The worst is to be blind to the very existence of frames and simply assume that you just see things as they are, and they can only be seen in one way, and everyone must also be seeing them in the same way. That is leadership ignorance.

Dealing with your demons

A few years back, I lived through a year of professional depression, spilling into my personal life, clouding my entire existence. I had no objective reason for it, my work was fine, my team was fine, I was appreciated, everything was, on paper, great and, yet, it all stopped meaning anything, it stopped being real.

I had been working with my team for years, actively engaged in their professional development, asking them to get better, leading by example. I had been doing it honestly, passionately and I could ask for a lot with a straight face, because I believed in it with all my heart and I was ready to do it first, to demonstrate it. I made mistakes, sure, but I was there, into it, giving it 110%. A lot of things made a lot of sense to me and I went to work every morning thinking about what I was going to do that day, full of energy, even on days when I was physically tired. I had always been ready to do anything that was needed, no matter the hour, no matter the job. My work was my house, that's how I saw it, and I cared about it in all possible ways.

And then, rather suddenly, it all stopped. All the dedication I had, all the things I had always done because they had to be done, they didn't seem obvious at all anymore. Doubt and emptiness flooded in. Why was I investing so much in my team? Why was I spending my time and energy trying really hard to teach these people all these things that, sometimes, it seemed like they didn't want to, or couldn't learn? Why was I doing all this, what for? Had I nothing more important to do with my life? Were all those late nights I spent writing some internal blog article, finishing some report, making sure it was all in order, really worth it? Was I really making a difference and was it a difference worth making? The only answer I could reach, the only answer I could believe, was "no".

My days became gray and everything I did felt dull and pointless. It wasn't aching pain, it wasn't a desire to scream, or to cry, it was just empty, and I constantly felt like I wanted to anything but what I was doing, be somewhere else, but mostly I just wanted to do nothing, to go to bed late, to wake up when I wanted to, to binge on YouTube, speak to nobody and be alone.

Depression is explained by some psychologists as an evolutionary adaptation to too much dedication. When you're too much into something, you lose perspective. Depression is, they say, a way to force you into some strategic thinking, and that it surely did for me.

Throughout that full year I was still mostly in control of my external manifestations, even if that control felt very tenuous and extremely tiring at times. I was aware of my condition, of my state of mind. I knew I need to do something. I gave myself the time to think and eventually I made a decision and I acted on it. I pushed through. I focused my attention, I changed my priorities on what matters. Step by step, I restarted. On a deeper level, I considered my mortality, my legacy and the meaning of it all, life, the world, my part in it. These weren't new thoughts to me, but it was the first time they were real, they were mine. Reading philosophy is one thing, living through those fundamental questions is another. It was a hard year, but in the end, I made it out of it stronger. Maybe it was my midlife crisis, not that it matters too much what it was.

I've worked with people that lived in fear, every day of their lives. I knew someone that always felt like he was struggling, at the limits of his skills, ready to crash, ready to fall, ready to be dismissed, rejected, fired. He was trapped in the Peter Principle, promoted one time too many, stuck in a job he couldn't really do, but that he could get close enough to scrape by for one more month, one more week, one more day. Every night he worked himself into bed. Every challenge, every situation, he was defensive, overwhelmed, focused on proving his worth, proving that he did his job, arguing, thinking small, without the mental space to think anything new, to act proactively, to take a chance. I can only imagine how difficult it must have been for him. Every time I saw him, he was startled, like a rabbit caught in headlights at night. He always looked like he was catching his breath, barely coping, surviving. In the end, he left his job and felt relief like he hadn't felt in a long time. I don't know what he did after that, but I hope he had the wisdom to step back and go back to doing the job he actually liked doing and that he was good at. There would be no shame in that. That's what his manager should have helped him see and do a long time before he did it out of sheer exhaustion and desperation.

I've also worked with people that were stressed out of their minds, as I was too, for months, during my year of sadness. I would wake up in the middle of the night, in cold sweat, because I had a nightmare about an email I had forgotten to send. A mail, a silly, stupid email, and nothing important for that matter. I developed insomnia, I couldn't go to sleep at normal hours, I stayed awake, unable to do much of anything else. I started having nightcaps, a shot of whiskey to put me to sleep. Sometimes it worked, sometimes I needed two, something that didn't work either. In the morning, getting up was a mess, I usually had just a few hours of sleep and I wouldn't be up to full speed until lunch. More than once I had to call in sick because I couldn't, despite the nightcaps, despite everything I tried, sleep. The night would come and pass, the sun would rise, it would be 8 AM and only then would I, suddenly, completely exhausted, crash. I learned a lot about the difference between work and stress during this time. I've always worked a lot, obsessively. As I write these lines, I'm at the end of a 15 hour work day, and I feel great. I'm tired, but I feel no stress, I feel no anxiety, nor have I felt it for a long time, not that kind of anxiety. I feel good, I feel great. Hard work is just hard work when you know why you do it and you're in control of what's happening to you and a hard day's work is nothing more than a guarantee of a good night's sleep. When, on the other hand, you feel like you're not in control and you're always chasing a moving target, and others determine your destiny, then you ruminate, you get stressed, you get anxious about all the little things and that's when it all gets very difficult, a downward spiral of loss of control leading to more stress leading to more loss of control.

Who do you talk about these things to? Your manager? If you're lucky, yes, a part of it at least, but you may not have a manager wise or trustworthy enough to share these troubles with. Most managers aren't. Your partner, if you have one. Your friends, although friends this close are also rare. Professional help, therapy maybe. If you're on your own, and even if you're not, you still need to lead your own recovery, focus on the small steps. Keep moving. Do something small. Clean your room. Plan your day. Eat better. Do some sport. Take control, that is key. Take control of something, of whatever you can, and expand from there.

What do you do if you're a manager and you sense some of your people are going through this kind of problems? Can you talk about it, can you open up the subject? Yes, you can. Don't assume and don't get more personal than you should but do ask. Tell them they seem stressed, are they ok? Can you help with anything? Don't try to be their parent, treat them like adults, but do offer the helping hand.

These things are hard to discuss and hard to go through, but they do happen and are not always easily visible from the outside. I know many people that have been through a depression like episode in their professional life, senior people, tough people, effective people, no snowflakes, and most people around them probably saw nothing different with them. I've eaten my own dog food, I did what I preach, I walked the talk and came out of it on my own, in stoic fashion, through self-reflection, discipline, small steps and plain old determination, but that worked for me. You may need something else.

Personality tests - worth it?

I mentioned my Big 5 score on the Agreeableness scale. The Big 5 Personality Traits are a system of describing one's nature and tendencies. There are dozens if not hundreds of personality tests out there, ranging from clinically controlled tests administered by a qualified psychologist all the way to quick Facebook quizzes. The personality test industry is a multi-billion dollar industry.

My opinion on personality tests is mixed. Taken too seriously, they are nothing more than a ludic fallacy, a way in which managers fool themselves with pretend science. Deciding careers and making promotion decision primarily off the back of personality tests is slightly, and only slightly better than astrology. It is abdication of management responsibility to look into somebody's eyes and tell her that you can't give her the job because of how she scored in the personality test. Out of the many tests out there, many are utter and proven crap. Some are potentially useful and some even might have some predictive value, as in, they might be, to some degree, useful in predicting future behavior in given situations. These are useful, but I only recommend them if you are wise enough to know what you're doing. Personality tests, even the good ones, even the ones you pay for and are done by professionals, they are not science, not remotely, not in the way math or physics are. They are, at best, a useful hint, a suggestion for you, as a leader, to integrate into a bigger picture and decide based on all the information you have at your disposal, out of which the personality test is only a part, and not the largest or most important part.

When it comes to your team, one good thing that can come out of the exercise of taking a personality test and discussing the results together is a better understanding that people are different. More empathy can come out of it, people may learn to better communicate and work with each other. They may also gain vocabulary and learn new words that describe feelings and states of mind, a useful thing as well. The danger is labeling. Human beings are ever in search of the answer, intolerant of the open question, and personality tests do give easy, seductive answers. Aha, one might say about her colleague, you are profile X, now it all makes sense, and, unconsciously, in the back of her mind, she's put her colleague in a box, she's stereotyped him.

I've used personality tests in my teams, but with heavy disclaimers and always as a tool for conversation, a reason to talk, never as an official part of a recruiting or performance process.

Step 2: Start strong, end well

In this step, we're going to look at both ends of a journey: how to start and how to end. How to begin an engagement, a job, a team, a relationship, but also how to close, how to decide when it's done, when it's time to end it, and do it well. We'll also look at the constant tension between determination and acceptance of failure: when is it right to persist in the face of hardship and when is it the time to accept that the chosen course of action is not going to work and we need to stop. I'll explore the idea of failure in detail, look at the differences between business failure and personal failure, why it hurts either way, how to deal with the hurt, learn what can be learned from it and to move on.

The first day

It's your first day in a new company. It's your first day as the team leader of a new team. It's your first day as the team leader of the team you've been a member of so far. It's the first day of a new project. It's your first day.

If you're an introvert, you'll be anxious about all the people you need to meet and all the first impressions you have to make. You'll want to plan and control the day as much as possible and you'll relish the time you have to spend with the IT guy, in a corner, setting up your password in silence.

If you're extrovert, you're looking forward to meeting and greeting, to making acquaintances, being nice, saying hi to as many people as possible.

In either case, the one thing you're unlikely to be thinking about is properly introducing yourself and setting the frame for your future collaboration of whatever you're starting there, and that is exactly what you need to do. Who are you? How do you like to work? How do you like to make decisions? What do they want? What do they think the problems are? What do you plan to start with? What needs to be done, what's the deadline?

You will avoid it because it will seem pretentious and arrogant. You will avoid it because the last thing you want to do on this overwhelming day is to take the initiative on something like this, but really, all you need is an hour, if that, sitting around a table with your new team, having a friendly conversation. This is not chest thumping, this is clarity and honesty. Introduce yourself on your first day, set everything on the right track. It may seem forced, unnecessary and rushed; it is not.

The day after I left my Endava job, on the first day of our consultancy business, I announced it on Facebook with a meme. It was the "coolest man on earth" meme and it said "It's not every day we start a business, but when we do, it's a great one". Underwhelming. Shy. Subtle beyond necessity. I can't redo that day, but I'm sure making up for it.

Make yourself known on your first day. Be authentic, be real. Don't expect rapturous applause, but do it nonetheless, it will help, and it will be appreciated.

Do it early, keep moving, stop the focus erosion

Most managers I know are not in control of their time. Their days are packed with recurring meetings and whatever they don't have allocated in advance they get taken from them by emergencies and fires they need to put out. They almost never get to think strategically and they have to take from their evenings just to keep up with emails. They're drinking from fire hoses. They don't get to be leaders, they get to be survivors.

A lot of the managers I know are not in control of their relationship with their teams. They don't feel they are able to speak the truth, or that they can honestly ask their team members for the kind of behavior and performance they would like to ask for. In this talent driven market they feel that people would just leave the company if they pushed them too much. More than that, deep down, more than leaving the company, or the team, they are afraid that their people would leave them. The illusion of respect is carefully preserved, through avoidance of conflict, rather than test the true depths of the relationship. Any non-narcissist leader goes through this fear, but all leaders need to move beyond it.

A lot of managers I know also don't have control of their relationships with their bosses. I'm not saying they're all passive and blindly obedient, but few really lead up the chain in a cohesive, proactive way. Their influence is diminished because of this.

A lot of the behavioral patterns that lead you down these unproductive paths start at the beginning, when you're new in a job and you make your first decisions that then become precedents and get repeated and reinforced until they become habits and expectations others now have from you. You're the new boss and your office manager comes to you asking you to review and approve a new supplier selection procedure. You think you shouldn't need to review this, you trust him with it, but you want to be a nice guy and you sit down and give it a read. You've just encouraged his approval seeking behavior and you've invested your time unwisely. It's easiest to say no the first time you get asked, it gets a little harder the second time because you've already done it once, and soon enough it's the way things are done. You can always decide to dive deep into something later on, but establish your default behavior carefully, don't get distracted, don't over commit and don't spread your focus too thinly. Say no. Say it politely, make sure people understand it's not personal, but don't be afraid to say no.

When I became a business unit manager for Endava, the big monthly routine I had to do was presenting the business unit report to the group executive team. I had been inducted in how that was done and I had seen how others business managers did it, but I wanted to do it differently. I spent the first 5 minutes of my first ever formal monthly business review telling the CEO and the other attendees how I wanted to present it, what I wanted to focus on, what I wanted to highlight and what I would focus less on. I asked if they had anything against that and told them that, obviously, at any point they wanted to hear more or less about something, they only had to ask. It was easiest for me, and for them if I said it straight out of the gate, rather than wait for 6 months before I did it.

It's your first weekly operational meeting with your team, your direct reports, and you go through the priorities for the week. One of them is repeatedly interrupting another one and keeps shutting him down. You don't like that, so you step in, you don't wait for 3 months to make sure. Maybe you don't need to make a huge deal about it just yet, but you do step in: interrupt the interrupter, give a voice to the interrupted, make sure he's heard, and they'll all see what you did, they'll know something more about you and you've just set one little precedent. Action speaks louder than words.

Take advantage of all beginnings, say no, protect your time and your focus, set precedents, make cultural statements, the start is the best time to do it. You can always do it later too, but it will be harder and, sometimes really hard. That's why so many professionals leave a job, sometimes a city, or even a country to get a fresh start, to get the chance to start anew and try not to repeat their mistakes. A big part of the fresh starts they're looking for tends to be in their heads, but that's sometimes harder to do than switching jobs.

As always, don't let this, or anything else, paralyze you into indecision. Yes, your first actions are important, but if you feel trapped by their importance to the level that you are stuck, unstuck yourself and just decide something. Movement is one of the great secrets of leadership, so keep moving. You almost never lose your focus as the result of one big blow or a major event, focus gets eroded one indecision at a time, in half an hour increments, usually coming to you in the form of meeting invitations. Make the time to step back, plan your week, remember what you're really trying to do, get out of the swamp, reduce and reject distractions, think strategically. At least once a week, get out of the office for an hour, go into the park, go to a coffee shop, put the phone away and think.

Be fearless

I had a colleague once and she was moving into a new position, a more senior position, which required a different skill set than what she was doing then, a big challenge, she was going to have to work really hard and, more importantly, take a lot of chances. She would have to expose herself to all kinds of new situations she would not be in control of or comfortable with, simply because they were new. As a senior developer and team leader, she was good at taking care of her team, organizing things, making sure work happened. As a manager with more direct client responsibilities, she would have to adjust her priorities and quickly learn how to have an impact in some very different types of situations. From concrete plans and tasks to the sometimes elusive and difficult to pin down "client satisfaction", especially when the client is a huge dysfunctional corporation, that's quite a daunting change, especially when it needs to happen quickly and in a high profile project. I was her manager and I was pushing and occasionally throwing her into situations that I knew were fundamentally safe, but not so safe as to not be real learning opportunities. She did remarkably well. She made her mistakes, she got some things wrong, but she had this one rare and precious quality: she was fearless. Whenever she had to do something she had never done before, the second she heard about it, she was already, mentally, there. Didn't know yet how to handle it, didn't know yet what to do, but she was there, already looking for options, whatever uncertainties or fears she might have had, she never let those stop or slow her down. That was, and I'm sure still is, an amazing quality of hers.

I've worked with people that were significantly more experienced than my colleague from above, but they were not fearless. People who are not fearless, when faced with a challenge, will sometimes feel an urge to articulate reasons to stick with the familiar and avoid the new, bogging down the process. I am not referring here to legitimate risk identification, but to emotional resistance to change, which makes it all harder, and less fun.

When I manage to be fearless it is not because I am not afraid, or that I don't feel any discomfort or anxiety. Courage and cowardness feel exactly the same, it's in the action where the difference lies. Fearlessness is not sticking to your comfort zone and repeating that which you already know, fearlessness is actually looking for terror, staring it right in the eyes, and stepping forward and giving it a little kiss. When I was choking at the very idea of speaking in front of a few colleagues, I decided to deep dive into my fears better than anyone has ever deep dived into their fears before. I made a project out of it. I registered for conferences, I made public promises that I would present this or that, so I couldn't back out of them, I excessively over prepared for some, then I underprepared for others. I tried it all. There was no quick and miraculous improvement, for months I would still uncontrollably sweat and feel sick in my stomach before every speech, but, step by step, it did get better, I got better and then, almost unexpectedly, on a given day, some good months later, I stepped up on some stage and I felt just fine. Loved it actually.

I made a project out of my fear and I went at it with all the discipline and determination I was capable of. I analyzed and solved it as I would analyze and solve any other challenge. Your big fears deserve a project plan. Do it. Pick one, plan it, do it. If you're not having at least a couple of hours of pure professional terror a week, you might want to worry about that.

Understand your new job

More than understanding the actual workings of a new role, some job changes need to be accompanied by a significant change in perspective. When I was a very technical senior developer, that was my frame and I judged everything through it. The question if we could do A or B hinged on the technical merits of A vs B and I would have chosen A because A was better. I may have looked at the immediate technical risk, but that was it. As a team leader I might have chosen A because my people knew A and there was no time to learn B. As an architect I also looked at the maintainability of the system and I might have chosen A because it was likeliest that there'd still be people in 5 years' time that we could hire to do the job. Later on, as a manager, I considered the costs as well. At even higher abstraction levels you consider transformative changes in the industry, the cultural impact of your decisions in your organization, competitive positioning, marketing, sales and so on. When I asked HR to hire people for my teams, I viewed myself as their internal client, I pushed my needs and asked for results, without really caring how they did it. When I became accountable for HR's results as well, I changed my perspective and I now looked at a bigger, more complex system, that included HR, which I couldn't treat as a black box anymore. When I viewed myself as a delivery guy, responsible for building things, I cared about building things right, in the right way. When I saw myself as a business person, responsible for selling solutions that solve clients' needs in a way in which they were willing to pay us for, I still cared about building things in the right way, but I also cared about building the right things at the right time.

Every change comes with the opportunity to slip. If you're a senior developer and you get promoted to team leader, don't use your new position to continue pushing your senior developer mindset and agenda, now with more authority. Understand the scope and perspective of your new job, internalize and adapt to the wider picture. Put the bigger hat on and fight the new fights, not the old ones.

Don't shave that yak

Shaving the yak is what we do when we worry too much and when we over plan. I read the yak story on a blog a long time ago and it goes like this. A man wants to take some pictures of his dog in the park, but he realizes he's left his camera at work (you can tell how old the story is, before smartphones). He gets into his car and starts driving to the office, but on the way there he remembers he doesn't have a key and it's the weekend, nobody's going to be there. He knows a co-worker who has a key, lives close by, could ask for it and return it right away. Only problem is, he once borrowed a coat from that co-worker, which he hasn't yet returned. The reason he didn't return the coat was that he tore it and he wanted to fix it before he took it back. He had found a tailor who could make it like new, but only if he brought the tailor some yak wool, out of which the coat was made. So that's why our man went to the zoo instead, jumped the fence and tried to shave a yak, getting arrested in the process, when all he started out to do was take some pictures of his dog. At least he did something, most of us only get to shaving the yak in our heads, from the safety of our couches.

We have our own, somewhat more aggressive version, in Romania. The rabbit wants to make pancakes and he needs to borrow a pan from the bear. He gets out and starts walking towards the bear's house, but on the way there he starts thinking. What if the bear will want some pancakes in exchange? That's fine, I'll give him a couple, it's only fair. But what if he wants 4? Hmm, there will be only 6 left for me. What if he wants 6, he's huge after all and eats a lot. But what if he wants 8? But what if he wants all of them? As he's thinking this, getting angrier and angrier, he's just ringing on the bear's door. The bear answers with a smile on his face: "Hey rabbit, what's up?", to which the rabbit responds, "Fuck you, fuck your pan and you can go fuck yourself!"

Just start. Just call the bear. Just ask for the key. The degree to which our worrying imagination can paralyze us from action is, pun intended, unimaginable. Just go do it.

Giving up too early

There are many ways to give up too soon and some are obvious but some more nuanced. Some people have a very specific idea about how work should be and they're very attached to it so they're brittle, inflexible, easy to upset. Not all stubbornness is bad, and some details are important enough to defend at all costs, but when you have too many of these things you care about, you are fragile. I've met people that quit jobs and projects over the silliest problems, from the hotel they were put in during a trip, to the kind of computer they were given, to how during their performance evaluation something wasn't said in a way in which they expected it, to how they were asked to do, temporarily, a type of work that wasn't their favorite, and I'm not talking about extreme situations. Sometimes, these breaking points are just the tip of the iceberg, the straw that broke the camel's back, coming on top of accumulated, uncommunicated and unaddressed frustration, so from the outside they look small, but from the inside they are just one more insult in a long line of mistreatment. Compassionate Radical Honesty, which I explore in the next step, will prevent the vast majority of these situations. Some other times though, people are just picky and touchy about all kinds of things, a frame of mind that is called big identity. You have a big identity when you identify yourself with a lot of things, not only core values and belief. You drive a certain car and you know exactly why that car is the best. You use a certain technology and you are sure it's the only rational choice. You are a fan of a particular football team and you are fanatical about it. You know what the absolute best place to go on vacation is. When you include all these things into what you perceive as your identity, you then feel attacked and even personally insulted when someone wants to buy a different car, or use another technology, or doesn't like football. The alternative is a small identity, composed out of the absolute key beliefs and values you hold dear, and everything else is just a choice. You like football, I like to run, who cares. We need to choose a technology for our next project, let's find the best one for the task, it's not personal.

I've also seen people that, again and again, engineer their own inevitable disappointment. They start a new job and they're feeling very good about it, everything is great, the people are great, the work is good, this is going to be awesome they tell you, and very different from the previous 5 jobs they held for less than a year each and said the exact same thing about in the beginning. Give it a few of months, and the first cracks start to appear. A couple of more months, and now they only talk to you about problems, about how they are giving it their best to fix them, but they can't seem to get traction, nobody understands them, and if they can't fix it, then they don't know what will happen they say, like it's ever a surprise. A few more months and they're practically on their way out, everything sucks, nobody wants to do anything real over there, it's a terrible company, and how much they've invested in it, how much they hoped, they were fools to do it, they say. Some do this because they are genuinely difficult, they have a big identity and they are very demanding, some others do it because they're lazy and this way they never have to do any real work and adapt to a situation and make something out of it, and some have an inflated opinion about themselves. One thing they all have in common is that they repeat this cycle again and again, off to the next naïve employer who's going to take them because, after all, they have quite a bit of interviewing experience and they make a good first impression.

When you find yourself complaining about something, ask yourself this question: are you complaining about it because you genuinely think it's a problem that needs fixing, or are you, deep down, complaining as a kind of defense mechanism? People can complain about a hard project because they really think they need better planning, or they can complain about it as a way to create excuses if they fail, a sort of pre-planned "I told you so". It's unprofessional to complain about something just to hide your weaknesses. Embrace your weaknesses, get better, ask for help, but don't try to make the whole project look bad just because you are uncomfortable about it.

When you find yourself ready to explode because of some small perceived slight, ask yourself why are you so upset by that one thing? Is it genuinely insulting, is it truly important, or is it just one more drop in a bucket of small frustrations you've been tolerating and keeping quiet about for a long time, hoping things would get better by themselves? If so, then fix that first. Compassionate Radical Honesty is, again, going to be your friend here. Are you legitimately reacting or are you overreacting? React maturely and proportionally to small problems as they come along, don't suffer in silence and let it all add up until you blow up.

Persistence is a key behavior when it comes to achieving any kind of success and it's hard enough to put in the work and dedication one needs for any serious project, to overcome the many legitimate obstacles, so don't sabotage yourself through emotional immaturity, diminishing your chances for no good reason whatsoever.

Stopping too late

There are two main reasons why people and groups keep at something way past the moment when they should have, rationally speaking, stopped: one is overconfidence, combined with the inability to see the warning signs, and the other is when they feel they can't afford to fail, combined with desperate effort to find any shred of hope and encouragement in whatever they can.

By the rational stopping point I mean that moment when the expected return of investment of your initiative, taking into account the likelihood of successful completion and all the costs involved, is smaller than the opportunity cost you're paying by persisting in it. There are, indeed, all kinds of legitimate reasons to act irrationally, by this definition at least, and most of them are of the personal kind: your need to prove something, to learn something, your defense of some value you believe in, some overarching life goal that is worth it for you, even if it ends up costing you everything, and all these are personal decisions nobody can really argue against. Not everything in life, or in work, needs to be pragmatic, but the one thing I think you really need to do is understand yourself. If you've made a conscious decision to keep going and you have deliberately decided against pragmatism, then that's fine and maybe even heroic, but understand what you're doing and make sure you're prepared to live with the consequences and don't end up bitter and upset at the world for something you did to yourself. The harder scenario is the delusion scenario, when you don't even realize how far off from the rational choice you are, when you are driven to illogical persistence by emotional and social forces that you don't even understand. As is typical with everything when it comes to our mind, there's no clear separation line and there's a lot of gray in the middle where, despite your best efforts, you might not know where you are: are you delusional or you determined? Should you stop or not?

Introspection, a Mental Sherlock, the things we discussed in the previous step, are going to be a great start, but there's more. Take for example a classic overconfidence scenario, the Bay of Pigs invasion by the US under President Kennedy in 1961. A CIA backed plan, it involved supporting a counter Castro force of Cuban rebels to go to Cuba, with the intention of overturning the communist regime. It was a spectacular failure and a post-mortem analysis revealed so many basic flaws in planning and assumptions that it bordered on the unbelievable. It's a classic case of groupthink, which is a group bias where otherwise capable, intelligent, qualified and dedicated people end up making bad decision after bad decision, apparently unable to really understand what they're doing. Lack of true communication, lack of debate and fear of conflict are the root causes of groupthink. In the Bay of Pigs situation, there was a CIA group of people that really wanted to do it and when they asked for analysis and the elaboration of a plan, they weren't really looking to be told it couldn't be done, they just wanted to know how, so every time someone raised a doubt, they would be bullied into silence. Meetings were of such format and recurrence that they didn't encourage dissenting opinions. The president was a supporter and personally involved, and frequently came to get updates, and that put pressure on the team, because nobody wanted to tell the president it couldn't be done, especially when everyone else was eager to say yes, sir. There's another famous example of 5 executives in a team that were about to make an acquisition decision where each of them thought the other 4 were for, when in fact none of them wanted to do it. This is called pluralistic ignorance, which is defined as *"a situation in which a majority of group members privately reject a norm, but incorrectly assume that most others accept it, and therefore go along with it"*. An idea, a proposal comes up, we look around and everyone else seems fine with it. We have questions, even basic questions, we have worries, but we assume that we must be missing something obvious since everyone else seems happy with it, so we say nothing, for fear of looking stupid. In the case of the 5 executives, the CEO decided, literally just before giving the final go ahead, to express some doubts. Encouraged by that, one by one, the others spoke too, and they realized they didn't want to do it, so they stopped. As the leader, you must create an environment where real debate is encouraged, and dissenting voices get to be heard and are not bullied into silence. You can inadvertently push your team into groupthink even with the best of intentions and with positive behavior. You are passionate about something, they can see you really want it, they don't want to disappoint you, so they ignore their own alarm bells to give you want you want. Yes, sometimes you want to motivate your team to do the impossible and your passion and determination is the example they need, but when you genuinely want their analysis and opinion on something you're unsure of, you might want to play it cool, even act like you don't have a preference, even if you do, so you don't pressure them into agreeing with you. The thing to remember about going too far due to overconfidence is that it doesn't require ignorance or incompetence. Competent, well motivated people can easily fall into this trap and it is far more common than we'd like to think. Looked at superficially, teams and decisions under the influence of groupthink seem logical: there will be data, sometimes a lot of data, there will be professionally looking reports, all written in serious business language. The problem will be in some key assumptions made in unrealistically positive terms, or some big risks ignored. The calculations themselves will be correct, but the input data will be flawed, and it will betray the groupthink. The best medicine and prevention is good leadership, combined with a culture of radical honesty.

Some other times people don't stop when they should because of the sunk cost bias, which is what we do when we say "we've invested so much in this, we can't give up now". The way to make a rational decision is to consider only what we can do from this point in time onwards, in order to influence the future, and how much we've already invested is not irrelevant, the past can't be changed, and it doesn't make sense to keep losing just because we've lost a lot already. On the other hand, looked at in terms of social and career costs, sunk cost bias is, in a way, rational. In most organizations, there will be a penalty for admitting failure so, unprofessional as it may be, there is a rational explanation for why weak leaders persist doing the wrong thing rather than stopping and regrouping: they don't want to be seen as having failed. Additional to this there is also social cost outside work, the fear of been seen as a failure by your family, your friends, your spouse, your kids.

None of these over commitment biases are good, as they make us blind to the irrationality of our persistence on a road we should stop following.

Domesticated failure and wild failure

Failure is a fascinating topic. In one, more mechanical sense of the word, failure is reaching too far, trying something outside your area of competence and falling short of the intended result, either through mistakes, or through insufficient return on investment. Looked at it in this way, in most creative businesses, in most situations, a certain degree of failure is good, because these environments demand that you constantly improve your product, your business, and you can't really do that if you only do what you know it's going to work, what you've already done before. You have to try new things, and new things come with the risk of failure. I call this kind of failure domesticated failure and it has been institutionalized in business processes such as Lean or Scrum and turned into a kind of controlled experimentation framework, where you have timeboxed intervals, usually few weeks logs, to attempt to do something, and you go at it in an 80/20 fashion: you're 80% confident you can do it, so the degree of unknown is relatively small. This kind of failure goes very well together with the experimentation mindset, where you set out hypotheses, in the form of plans, give yourself a box of time and resources to test them out, to execute the plan, and then you stop and see what worked and what didn't, learn you lessons and move on to the next experiment and the next box. It is no accident that Scrum and all these frameworks try really hard to demystify and sanitize failure, control it and make it look like it's no big deal, because they understand human psychology and understand that otherwise competent people will find it very difficult to admit and discuss their own failures, and learn from them, so they go the extra mile to make that as easy as possible. It's a kind of getting out of the failure closet, and yet, it's the hardest thing to get right. You'll see Scrum working in all its other aspects but the retrospective meeting, the meeting at the end of the box, or sprint as they call it, where the team should meet and discuss what went well and what went wrong. If this meeting happens at all, it rarely gets to the real conversation, which is individuals identifying and admitting individual failure, saying "I made this mistake, and this is what I learned from it".

Domesticated failure is mostly a systems thing, it's about frameworks and processes that standardize your experimentation mindset as a team or as a company. Wild failure, on the other hand, is deeply personal and it can be so painful that it feels like death and the way out like mourning. It's the kind of thing that's all about you, keeps you up a night, makes you feel like crap, makes you stare into the mirror not knowing what you're looking at. It's that sinking feeling when suddenly you wonder if the last few years of your life are worth anything, if you're really capable of doing anything important at all, if you should even try anymore or just give up. What you thought was solid ground turns to sand and all your mental constructions of who you are and what you do withers away as you reckon with the implications of your failure.

In order to experience wild failure, you have to push yourself really hard, go far outside your comfort zone. Bad things happening to you are not the same as failure. Painful and tragic as they may be, they feel different. Failure is a deliberate attempt at something that goes wrong, it's not simply bad luck hitting you as you were just minding your business.

You quit your job and start your own business. A year later, you've invested all your savings, you've borrowed from friends and family and you're still not close to success. It's not a total failure, that would be easier to see. You've built something, you've achieved some things, you've moved forward, progress has been made. It's not close to where you hoped you would be by this time, but you also realize that your initial expectations were unrealistic. Is it a failure? You've made many mistakes along the way, sure, but looking back, was there really any other way to learn? You have no problems acknowledging these intermediate failures, learning from them, adjusting, but the big question of keep going or give up, what do you do about that? On one hand, you now know that it couldn't have worked in a year, so giving up now is the same as ensuring failure. On the other hand, it could have gone a lot better, and you've already depleted most of your resources. Maybe this is not the thing to stand your ground on, maybe your energy would be better invested in something else? Do you even have enough energy left for another try at something else? One of the problems you have is that there is no clear standard to compare yourself with. There are examples out there of much faster success but there are also examples of startups that persisted for 5, 10 years in the face of hardship, only to then explode. There are lessons in all of those stories, but none of them applies to you wholly, you can pick any of them and say "this is me", all you have to do is believe it. It's a tricky situation you're in, you're not only under a lot of pressure, but you're also unsure about what to expect, what failure is, what you should do. There's no boss coming in and telling you that in order to get to the next seniority level you have to do this and that. There's no one setting objectives for you, there's no predefined path to take. Some people that have done this say that you should set some clear objectives before you even start, so when you are, a year or two down the road, in the fog of war, uncertain about what is what, you can look back at your original objectives and decide based on that. It's a bit like going to the casino and deciding upfront, before leaving home, that you're only going to gamble a set amount of money, no matter what happens, how excited you get, how promising it seems once you get into it. Once you're in the thick of it, you can easily lose perspective and escalate your commitment again and again, against all rational thinking. In a sense, I'm talking about putting your business in a box and not letting it consume your entire existence, so you can hope to keep an objective perspective on it, look at it from the outside and make logical decisions. This is really hard to do, as you also need, at the same time, to be really dedicated and into it, obsessed even, if you're to make it a success, because this kind of thing really doesn't work unless you give it your best. Let's say that you decide, after two years of hard work, to stop. Why did you stop? Looked at it through Jeff Bezos' regret minimization framework, how are you likely to feel about stopping when you're 80 and on your death bed? Are you going to be content that you gave it your absolute best, until you could objectively no longer keep going, or are you going to regret that you were weak and gave up before you should have? Did you stop for the wrong reason? Did you stop because you were worried about what people were going to say about you? One easy lesson to remember is that if you're considering giving up, take a couple of days, get out of the office, get some perspective, talk to some people, remove yourself from the immediate pain.

In my experience, once you get into something big and important, like starting your own business, once you get past the initial exploration phase and you start investing for real, it then becomes much harder to stop and you're more likely to go too far rather than stop too early. There is no absolute right or wrong here, if you want to burn all your savings on some long shot idea, do it, but the one thing I can recommend to anyone is the self-awareness to understand why you're doing what you're doing, and to make sure you're doing it for the right reasons and you're comfortable with the decisions you've made.

Regardless of why and how you and admit failure, what follows after is going to be hard, because the thing that you just failed at has consumed the vast majority of your waking hours for a long time, that's where you've had your emotional highlights, it was a big part of you, so when it stops, you find yourself staring at an empty space that used to be you and it's now gone. What are you going to fill it with? You will enjoy the peace and quiet, yes, but that is small comfort for the looming terror of being forced to spend so much time with yourself and come to terms with your failure and your identity. It's no wonder that many people need to fill this space with something, whatever, just so they don't have to think about it. A relationship ends, a new one is immediately started, just to validate one's ego keep the distracted, keep them away from thinking. A business crashes, a new one is started immediately. Moving on is great and you should do it before too long, but before that do spend some time to wallow in your pain. It's priceless learning and it's the stuff of life.

Step 3: The miracle of compassionate radical honesty

Caring effectively

As I write this, there are IT professionals here in Iaşi, some of them very senior, in the process of receiving heartbreaking feedback going to the core of their performance and professional identity. They are being told that large parts of their attitude and delivery are unsuitable for the expectations of their job and that they must drastically change or leave. The reason this is happening is that, for years in some cases, the bosses of these people did not do anything to address and fix a situation that was painfully obvious to them. They hoped, they hinted, they avoided, they worked around it. In their desire to avoid conflict, or because of their misguided empathy, they let situations fester until they could no longer be ignored and way past beyond the point when an easy fix might have been possible. I also have been guilty of this, and in that, I failed as a leader. It is always the responsibility of the leader to address performance problems, and always her fault if they are left to worsen. The temptation to just let it go, to hope it will get better, to maintain the apparent harmony, to move on, is always there, for all of us. It is a mistake. It is also true that some people are particularly difficult; most others in their place would just have realized they weren't doing well, they would have gotten the hints, they would have shown more self awareness, they would have fixed something, they might have left themselves. This is no excuse for the leader and it is always a leadership failure when direct feedback is avoided, and unsustainable situations are left to exist and develop. Avoidance out of weakness is leadership failure. Leaders can show wisdom by avoiding some conflict and showing tact in some situations, but never when they do it out of fear or misguided goodness, and in the process neglecting the needs and priorities of the team and the company. Teams and companies are routinely wrecked because leaders do not have the strength to give the kind of fast, direct, unfiltered feedback that keeps people honest and expectations clear.

Nothing wrong with being a nice guy, but if that comes at the cost of leadership effectiveness, it's a disaster.

I remember precisely the day when I realized exactly what I needed to do avoid this.

I was working with a company and a situation was brought to my attention: a project manager was driving everyone very hard, too hard. He had been having conflict with everyone in his team and beyond, again and again. The situation was getting out of hand and the team was under risk of imploding. I always say conflict is great, as a way of keeping us honest, but when one person is at odds with pretty much everyone around him, and it's getting worse by the day, the situation deserves careful and immediate attention. His manager had spoken to him several times about it, but there was never any noticeable improvement. He was driven and determined for the best of reasons: to deliver. He was smart, fast, very good at his job and had little patience for whatever he perceived as insufficient performance. Problem was, he perceived almost everything as insufficient performance and he had difficulties in seeing anything from any point of view other than his own. He could argue anything away, and aggressively so. It was his way or the highway and unjustly so, as most of the people around him were doing their best and his criticism of their work and attitude was frequently unfair. I was asked to help, to intervene, to convince him that he needed to change his ways. I said yes.

I already knew three key things about him. One, he had good intentions. Based on everything I knew, his drive was to deliver the project successfully. Sure, he was also out to prove himself, but we weren't going to hold that against him. Two, we couldn't fault him for his skills, he was doing, in a technical sense, good work and working hard. Even his aggressiveness was, at its core, in my mind, a positive. Three, and therein lay the problem, he saw the world his way and his way only. His first reaction to any kind of feedback was to ferociously argue it away. It was always somebody else that did something wrong, or they didn't get it, or, when he failed, the context was unwinnable, nobody else could have done a better job. Taken superficially, his arguments could seem logical and always had a portion of truth in them, and he did believe in what he was saying, but the fact remained, and this was key to everything, that he was uncoachable and that meant that he couldn't be helped to improve his performance.

At first, I started to prepare my talk with him under familiar lines: I would lay out the situation, exemplify some incidents, present the impact of his actions on others, ask for his view, listen to it carefully, present alternatives, suggest changes, all while being calm, impersonal, professional. I spent about 20 minutes planning this in my head when I suddenly realized I was lying to myself. It wasn't going to work. I was going to end up in a long, protracted conversation where he would argue away everything I had to say, I would try to say again, in a different way, he would argue it right back, we would run over time, reach no conclusion and he would likely leave the room happier with himself then when he entered, successfully having faced another challenge to his worldview. I would stay behind, having agreed on some diluted promise of "trying our best", deep down knowing I have achieving nothing. Nobody would have blamed me, that's how things are done in these situations, and I was definitely able to do it competently. If it wasn't going to work it wasn't because of me, it was, well life. The situation. But this time I wasn't going to have that happen. I simply wasn't willing to invest my time and energy intro a corporate ritual of bland management with slim chances of real change. I decided to drop my plan and instead do something else entirely. Something that not only had a better chance of working, but would also be faster, easier, and definitely more fun. I entered the room and told him right away I wasn't interested in anything he had to say. I would speak for 10 minutes and then leave, and he would do whatever he wanted to do with what I had would say to him. He didn't even have to stay and listen to me, the door was right there, but he did stay. I drew a circle on the whiteboard. He was in the middle and around him 12 or so people he was regularly butting heads with. Team leaders, developers, collaborators of the team, men and women, senior and junior. I then told him that this was a mathematical improbability. He had bad relationships with all and they, in general, had good relationships with each other. I told him that no matter how well he could argue any particular incident, he couldn't argue with math and, unless he wanted to claim a conspiracy, the situation simply wasn't sustainable. I told him I heard he was an excellent project manager, but this wasn't working. Why was he pissing everyone off, making his work that much harder in the process? Was the current situation to his advantage? Was he increasing his influence by behaving in this way? Was the fact that he always argued anything his way and that he always thought he was right going to change the objective reality of his failing professional relationships? Was he going towards success or, maybe, just maybe, did he need to change something? Was he willing to consider that possibility? These are my thoughts, I told him in closing, you do what you want, and you will live with the consequences. Not because I say so, not because I want to impose my view on you, but because reality can not be argued with and there will come a point when steps will have to be taken to protect the project and the team, and by that time it will be too late for debating why someone did or didn't do something, or that it was actually someone else's fault or that everybody else got it wrong. The time for arguments will have passed. I then thanked him for listening and left the room. If at this point your first thought is "I'd like to be able to do things like that, but my company/boss won't let me", you're kidding yourself. You can do it.

Why did I do it? I've never found it difficult to be direct and blunt, but this was different. My Mental Sherlock kicked in and suddenly I could clearly see myself in the situation, the choices I had, the paths in front of me. I had been blunt many times before, my whole life basically, more or less. I always had a measure of control over it, sometimes complete control. Instinctively, I always did my best to do it in a way that didn't attack the person as a human being. I had a feeling that it had a way of working, that it cut through the crap, that it could unblock situations and make people listen in way that they could actually even appreciate the brutal honesty, but it was always murky, a blunt instrument, something I was unsure of. Many of the ingredients were already there, but there was no chef. I was cooking a meal without an understanding of how heat works, until that day it is, until just before that meeting, when I suddenly realized what it was, how powerful it was, and how much I loved doing it. It was my first taste of what I now call Compassionate Radical Honesty and there was no stepping back. When the meeting was over, instead of the corporate powerlessness I would have felt if I had taken the traditional way of addressing the problem, I was busy promising to myself that I would never go back to being boring again and, from that moment on, I would always employ Compassionate Radical Honesty. I didn't have a name for it then, the name came a few years later, but I already knew enough.

Honesty, because if we have to choose, we always choose truth over feelings. Radical, because we say truths that they haven't heard in a long time, or maybe never, and we're ready for the reactions and emotions that may come out of it. Compassionate, because we're not brutes: we're never blunt just for the sake of it, this is not a power trip, we do it with the full intention of helping. Radical Honesty is not a way to care less, from the contrary, it's a way to care more and more effectively. Was there any moment during my conversation with the manager above where I did not hope for a successful outcome, for him? No, there was not. Was I doing exactly what I thought had the highest chance of helping him? Yes, I was. Was I locked in a win-lose dynamic where I felt he was my adversary and I had to win? Not for a second. Far from making me care less, Compassionate Radical Honesty was allowing me to care effectively.

Stone age hardware

More than one school of psychology looks at the politeness vs sincerity conflict as one of our core conflicts. Politeness is when we censor ourselves for the sake of others. We do it when we are afraid, we also do it when we want to protect. Sincerity is when we speak the truth, relationships and feelings be damned. Life is a complicated balancing act between these two and this tension can consume us. Truth is liberating, forced politeness is suffocating. Being too polite can not only ruin a project, a team, a culture, a company, but also our sanity.

Why is it so difficult to speak the truth? Yes, sometimes we face objectives consequences, like the fear of losing our job at a time where we can't afford to lose it, but even when that is not the case and we are, objectively speaking, safe from any serious consequence, most of us will still find a million other reasons to not speak up and choose short term harmony instead. Why is that?

The answer is old, very old, imagine a dark forest at dusk kind of old. Big trees, dense undergrowth, for miles and miles around. You and your few fellow travelers, armed with spears, coming from your unsuccessful hunt, tired, hungry, on your way back to your cave. As you slowly and carefully make your way, you hear the loud snap of a branch breaking behind some big bushes to your left, 30 or so meters away. You freeze in your tracks and look, trying to figure out what it is. You don't see anything, but you can hear a ruffle behind the bush and it seems like it could, maybe, be a big animal. You now have a choice. If it's a deer, that could be dinner, and your family's dinner, and what a dinner. If it's a boar, that could be dinner too, although a more dangerous kind. If it's a bear, it might mean your death. Or, it could be the wind, a passing hare, or a bird. What do you do? If you leave without investigating, you could miss a potentially juicy opportunity. If you check it out, you could end up hurt, or dead. In that scenario, as it turns out, your choice is easy. If you can't figure it out from a safe distance, you leave. If there's a 90% chance that dinner is behind that bush, and a 10% chance of it being a bear, but the consequence of that 10% is fatal, then you never take the chance. You leave. In other words, you accept false negatives, and you let opportunities slide, for the desire of avoiding risk, because risk is of a very serious nature.

What about standing up in front of your tribe at the evening fire and stating a brave, innovative and controversial opinion on some important issue? What could be the consequence of that? Is there a 5% chance of you being casted out of the tribe? Is there a 3% chance of someone challenging you right there and then to a fight to the death? 5% might not seem like much, but the consequence of that 5% is dire. So, again, you think really carefully before standing up and having an unusual opinion.

What if you're out gathering berries on the outskirts of the forest, and you suddenly spot a couple of strangers on the side of the nearby river. Your small band lives in a sparsely populated area, actually, the entire world is sparsely populated. You don't see people outside your band more than once a year maybe and when it happens there's always a risk of the encounter turning violent. You abandon your berry gathering and immediately run back to your group, to tell them about the strangers. Strangers are dangerous until proven otherwise.

We've evolved to stay away from danger, and the stranger. A minority of us, the risk takers, the teenagers, like to get closer and closer to the fire, but generally speaking, when something is unsure, it's better to leave it unknown, rather than end up accidentally poking a bear. Going to sleep on an empty belly is unpleasant, but survivable, for quite a few nights in a row if you have to, and preferable to a violent bear encounter. The problem comes in how animals, including us, learn things. How exactly do we do know, as a species, to fear big animals with big claws and scary teeth? We don't know it intellectually, that's not how we primarily know it. We know it instinctively. When we hear an unexpected noise at night in a dark alley, the adrenaline rush is instantaneous, we don't wait to calmly assess the situation and calculate the odds of danger. Our instincts take over and we're in fight, flight or freeze mode. The process is traumatic, exhausting. We don't want to go through it if we can avoid it, even if it turns out to be nothing. That kind of scare is not pleasant, not for most of us.

Take these instincts and put them in the modern world and they start giving all kinds of false alarms. Imagine yourself at a cocktail party. You have people around and every one of them is like a bush and there might be either a deer, a bear, or nothing hiding behind. Every one of them is like that stranger on the side of the river. Let's say there is a 33%-33%-33% chance that, if approached, any one of the people at that party will be sympathetic, dismissive or indifferent to whatever you have to say to them. Our instincts are very afraid of that 33% chance of dismissal. They treat it like they would treat a bear, but the situation is completely different. What is the cost of dismissal? The prehistoric bear was a mortal danger, but the price you pay for the metaphorical bear encounter of someone not agreeing with you, not buying from you, not liking you is so small it's, for all practical purposes, zero. So, if you're at a business event and your job is to see what's behind every tree, you should bravely go ahead and check, because any number of "bears" you may find are probably

going to cost you a big fat nothing: a simple, usually polite, almost always non permanent rejection. On the other hand, the cost of not even trying, of not finding that one or two people that may end up being valuable business partners, that is very high. The equation is entirely reversed from our prehistoric times: the cost of accepting the false negative is much higher than the cost of avoiding a potential positive. Missing opportunities is, in our modern world, much worse than not trying at all and yet, as simple as this fact may be to understand, we still get knots in our guts when we go and say "hi" to a stranger at a party. We still shake uncontrollably when we go up on a stage to hold a speech, as if our tribe was still prone to casing us out into the desert, to wander alone and starve, as punishment for our impertinence. The reason for this is that our brains still haven't had a chance to evolve and adapt. A few thousand years are not enough, biologically speaking, to adapt to the new reality and our instincts are still old and hardwired. What we intellectually know, we don't yet intuitively know. We have 21st century educations and life experiences, but they're running on stone age hardware.
Psychologists call this the reptilian brain, or system 1, the primitive part of our brain, the subconscious reactions. It happens without the cortex wanting it or controlling it.

This is the root of our inner tension between sincerity and politeness. Our rational mind expects one thing, doesn't understand why and how the primitive brain underneath it wants something else, internal tension is not understood or reconciled, frustration, anger, sadness ensue. We are unhappy with our actions, perpetually chastising ourselves for not being as brave or, more specifically, as honest as we'd like to be. When am I going to be able to tell my boss that I am unhappy with the work? When I am going to be able to tell my people exactly what I want from them? You want to, you start the conversation, and then it all melts into some generic statement that don't say much at all. I've told you why this happens, but, more importantly, how can you change it?

There is a way out of this corner. The Mental Sherlock is the self awareness mechanism that lets us see, understand and, in time, with enough practice, control and diminish our instinctive reactions. Compassionate Radical Honesty is the tool that we use to speak the truth. When I was terrified of public speaking, sweating profusely, ready to puke, choking, unable to remember my name at times, I kept doing it. I employed my Mental Sherlock, I analyzed my reactions, found experiments and challenges, learned, did it again, and again, and again. I never had a doubt that I could do it, because there are examples all around us of people learning to control their fight, flight or freeze reaction. Firemen run into fires and there's nothing evolutionary about that. Soldiers run into bullets. Pilots fly, the most unnatural of human acts. With sufficient understanding and adequate practice, anything can be learned. If a soldier can learn the fatally unnatural act of jumping on a grenade to save his mates, I could surely learn to stand on a stage and say some words with a minimum of eloquence and without feeling like I wanted to disappear into the ground. And I did.

What Radical Honesty is and isn't

There's this 1997 movie, called "Liar Liar", where this sleazy, lying, cheapskate lawyer, played by Jim Carrey, is forced, by magic, to speak the truth for 24 hours. Hilarity ensues as he is compelled to blurt out the most shocking, embarrassing and silly truths to everyone he meets, from admitting past lies out of the blue to saying how he hates something someone is wearing. This is not what I mean by radical honesty. Radical honesty is not about speaking unnecessary little truths or criticizing irrelevant aspects for no reason whatsoever. It's not about feeling compelled to say the coffee sucks if the coffee sucks, or always having an opinion about every little thing that comes up in the conversation. That's not being honest, that's being obnoxious. Radical honesty is about speaking your mind, considerately but plainly and directly, in those things that matter, or when your opinion is requested on something important.

Radical honesty is also not the opposite of lying. Simply not lying is not enough. Radical Honesty is speaking your mind, on the things that matter, as if you were not afraid of anything, even if you are. You tell it how it is, you call it how you see it, plainly put, no matter who asks you, no matter if they'd like to hear it or not, no matter if what you say is going to be popular or controversial. If you look at a team and you see a bad relationship between two team members that are always fighting, but nobody says anything about it, you call it out: "I sense a tension between you two, is that impacting your decisions?". If you work with someone not performing or not delivering on their commitments, you clearly restate your expectations and give them direct, honest feedback. You don't avoid conflict and you don't leave the situation unresolved.

The most direct application of radical honesty, other than with yourself, is with your people, with your team. You have to tell them, now and frequently, everything important that you're thinking about them. Tell them what you like about them and tell them what you don't. Tell them where you see them in the big scheme of things, how do you forecast their growth. Make sure they know what you're thinking, and know it now, not in some future when you'll find the so called right time to tell them. Make your expectations clear and your feedback unmistakable. I made many mistakes with this, especially early in my management career, when I was avoiding telling the full truth, because I wanted to be nice, because I wanted to only encourage and never say something bad. I now know that radical honesty is encouragement and while it may not always be nice, it is fair, it is just, and it is necessary. You're not doing anyone a favor by leaving them in the blind. First time I was responsible for someone, when I was told I was going to be the people manager for two new hires, responsible for their performance evaluations, I took it very seriously and I was extremely hands-on in their induction and training. One of them was very good and things went easy. The other one was slow, difficult, and I ended up making the mistake all new managers make, which is investing more time in the difficult ones than in the ones ready, eager and able to learn. I had to make this guy ok too, I had to get him across the line, I couldn't fail, that was my thinking. The problem was that, although I knew exactly what he did wrong, which was in his attitude, it never crossed my mind that I could tell him that, that I could simply tell him that he's too defensive, spends too much time and energy trying to look smart rather than getting smart. He wasn't the quickest anyway, but his attitude towards learning was what was holding him back the most. I didn't know I could just tell him that, as my opinion, as my feedback. Instead, we had these long, awkward conversations, where we only addressed the content, the thing I had given him to do, without ever talking about the way he was doing it. I got him across the line, with extraordinary effort, and he became an ok employee, but nothing more than that, and not the most pleasant to work with either. There's nothing wrong in and by itself with having difficult people in your team, if it's the right kind of difficult, if it's the difficulty of unlocking significant potential, the difficulty of brilliant eccentricity, but not the difficulty of trying to help someone that can't or doesn't want to be helped. Regardless of what kind of difficult you have to deal with, or no difficulty at all, radical honesty is golden, but back then I didn't know how to do it. I shied away from it because I didn't want to be too directive, too constraining. I did not know that clarity and autonomy can and do coexist just fine. I was avoiding conflict, and not out of fear of conflict itself, but out of a deeper fear of being disappointed. As long as I didn't precisely ask for what I wanted, I only hinted at it in vague terms and as a long term goal, I could go on believing they would get there. And no, there's nothing wrong with believing in the best possible version of your people and telling them to shoot for the stars. The only thing I regret is avoidance. I avoided clarity because I didn't want them to fail. That was a mistake, because clarity is not incompatible with high expectations, the opposite is true. No micromanagement, no over controlling, just clarity and honesty.

Another type of important radical honesty is with those that want things from you, such as you bosses, or your clients. Do they clearly understand what you can do for them, and what you can't? I believe in the professional duty to volunteer enough information to clarify the matter at hand, even if you weren't directly asked all the relevant questions. If you're asked if you can do X and you can get away by saying "yes", but you know Y will also be needed for the intended final result, and for whatever reason you're worried about Y, even if it's not your direct responsibility, say it. Volunteer enough context to make sure you understand and to make yourself understood. When something is not possible, say so. When you need something, ask for it.

The doctor syndrome

Some leaders, especially beginner leaders, think they're doctors, and they've taken the Hippocratic Oath. They think they're there to save everyone, no matter what, no matter how. What they forget is that they are not curing patients nor are they working with children. We work with willing adults who are engaged in a voluntary work contract. We owe them honesty, we owe them fairness, we owe them many things, but if the adult across the table from us doesn't want to behave like an adult and fundamentally doesn't want to be here, then he shouldn't be here. We are not doctors, we're not here to "save" people. The team, not any individual, is your highest priority. Beware of the doctor syndrome.

The one operating principles of Radical Honesty

Let me repeat the overall definition of Compassionate Radical Honesty. We have honesty, because if we have to choose, and we will have to choose every day, we always choose truth over feelings. We are radical, because if we have to we say truths that they haven't heard in a long time and we're ready for the reactions and emotions that may come out of it. We are compassionate, because we're not brutes: we're never blunt just for the sake of it, this is not a power trip, we do it with the full intention of helping, if help is possible.

How does this look on a day by day basis? How do you apply it in your team, in every meeting, in every interaction, in every situation? There is just one principle you need to follow: voluntarily tell your people where you stand.

That's it. You say what needs to be said, clearly, and you volunteer the information relevant to the situation, even if you're not precisely asked. It eliminates obscurity, people don't have to get information out of you with a claw. You're not passive aggressive, you're not driven by petty emotions, only speaking out on some things and not others, you're not manipulating the conversation, you're not derailing the agenda. You are focused on the common good, you say what needs to be said clearly, people understand your opinion, they know where you stand. If you're not directly asked or if there's no formal process or slot for you to say your piece, you find a way to volunteer your information and opinions to the relevant people. As a leader, you are a voluntary radiator of information. You continuously share your thoughts on the team's journey, on progress, on obstacles. Of particular importance is that your people know where you stand in relation to them, or, better said, where they stand in your eyes. They should never have to wonder if you think they're doing a good job or not, if they're making progress or not. Use your 1-1s and all other means to make sure that your opinion on their performance, professional behavior and growth is, at all times, crystal clear to them.

Wherever you go, whatever meeting you attend, whatever person you're talking to, ask yourself this: do they know where I stand? Do they know generally where I stand, and do they know where I stand on this particular issue, the topic of this conversation? If you have doubts, make sure.

Think of the best leaders you know, the great political leaders, the great business icons, your personal role models: do you not very clearly know exactly where they stand on the major issues relevant to their field, what they wanted to achieve, what they fought for, how they liked to act? Of course you do, it's part of what makes them great. That is your goal as well, when your people think about you, they should know where your stand.

Cultural differences

From July 2005 until January 2007 I lived and worked in India. I turned down an offer here in Iași that was almost three times my salary at that time and I chose to stay with my current company, and take a 6 months India assignment, as a software architect, to work with the teams there on designing the new version of our product, and also help with the communication between the Pune and Iași teams. 6 months turned into 12, and then 12 turned into 18. I went there at a period in my life where I had all the obsession for software perfection of young age and little to no interest in anything else. I wasn't a general asshole, I was ready to help, available, generous with my time, but when it came to any technical debate, I would instantly catch fire and I would see every conversation as a battle to be won, arguments as my ammo. I was terrible at listening. That was me when I left for India, on the first flight of my life, connection through Rome if I remember well. I landed in Mumbai late at night and the moment I left the air-conditioned area I hit a humid hotness of a kind I've never felt before. A car was waiting for me and we started the 3 hour drive to Pune with me in the back, eyes glued to the endless rows of palm tree and homeless people sleeping on the sidewalks as we were getting out of the massive, dusty steamy megalopolis Mumbai was and probably still is. India has enough to scare you for life in the first 10 minutes, but, if you're of a certain attitude and you can see past that, it also has enough to love it forever. I reached Pune, got into my apartment, figured out a way to order some food, ordered prawns with some kind of lemon sauce and ate them fully, beaks and all. Chewy I thought, but I was too tired to doubt it, so I chewed. In the end, my time spent in India ended up being the most important period of self discovery in my life, because of my solitude, my work, my travels, my reading, my writing, drugs and everything in between. On most nights it took hours to go to sleep, chain smoking Mildsevens with a bottle of Jack, trying to write poetry, listening to 70's rock. I crashed at 3, or 4, woke up at 9 or 10, showered and went to work. My typical work day was 11 am to 11 pm and it was all encompassing, crushingly intensive. I gave it my best, there was nothing else I wanted to do but exhaust myself in everything I did.

Fundamentally, my Indian colleagues were the same as me. Nice guys and girls trying to do their best, young crowd, building a career, eager to learn. When it came to their appetite for confrontation however, I found most of them remarkably different, and it started with the little things. When we went out for dinner, it invariably started with a 15 minute conversation about what we should order, as the local custom was get a few big portions of something on some big trays in the middle and to share. I didn't mind the sharing per se, but I disliked the collective decision making; I wanted to eat what I wanted to eat, I didn't want to change my preference because of someone else, I didn't want to spend the brain cycles trying to reach some agreement on something I had no interest in even discussing. I tended to be the odd one out and order my own thing. When about a dozen of us went to see Rang De Basanti, a movie about corruption in the Indian Air Force and a social phenomenon for talking plainly about it, I watched it, ate my popcorn, drank my coke, liked it, took a cab and went home. The next day an email chain started among those of us that had been to the theater the night before: *"What a beautiful patriotic movie"* one said. *"Yes, it teaches us how to love our country another replied"*. It took me 4 or 5 replies to figure out they weren't kidding, and they were, in fact, serious. Yes, they had reasons to feel the message of the movie much more than I did, being about their country and their issues, but that side, I couldn't imagine any kind of movie, no matter how well made, no matter how emotional, no matter how impactful, that would make me or almost any other Romanian I knew email those kind of messages, in that way, that early in the morning to boot. My Indian colleagues were just too sweet. Almost any idea I would propose, they would embrace. I loved them, don't get me wrong, and I met some razor sharp individuals over there and many of them left an indelible mark on me. I can clearly and vividly see their faces even now and I'm getting emotional just writing about it, but nonetheless, their lack of cynicism was discomforting. Optimism is great as a dominant trait, but no angst whatsoever, no fuck you, no nothing? At points, it felt like I was part of an experiment in agreement: how many yeses can we squeeze into a typical working day?

How would I apply Compassionate Radical Honesty in a team like that, from a different culture, if I were given one to manage today? Not that differently from how I would do it here, or anywhere else, but there are some differences. As a manager, the main challenge wouldn't be telling them what to do or telling them what I liked and disliked about their work, that was in many ways easier to do over there than here. The big thing would be figuring out how to engage them in lively dialogue, in confrontation, have them shoot back, so we could, at the end of the day, reach deep and meaningful agreement, having thoroughly discussed all the delicate issues. While cognizant of national culture, I wouldn't get stuck in it. There's loads I don't like about Romanian culture and work ethic as a whole, but I don't work with "Romania" and I wouldn't be working with "India", which, strictly from the point of view of this conversation, are not much more than loose abstractions. I would be working with specific people, with individuals, and a small number of those people, under 10, would be my direct reports and I would select them carefully. I would set, with each and as a team, clear expectations of behavior, during the hiring process and after. I would, for a while at least, preface and close my CRH spikes with little explanations, I would be more explicit than usual, I would make absolutely sure that my messages and the intent of my messages is clear. You know, I would talk about the talk, before actually having the talk. "I'm about to ask you to do something you may not have been asked before, and you may find it strange, but hear me out"; this kind of setting the scene can help a lot.

Cultural differences are important, but they are sometimes overrated because people get too precious about them. For everything related to history, politics, religion, social norms and habits, stay out of it, unless you know what you're doing. At work however, create a professional context with clear rules, allowing people to interact under the norms of that place, not under the background norms of whatever they do outside. Adapt some of your practical habits to the location, but not all. Be explicit, be clear, repeat, be humble but direct, explain yourself, decide, do, learn, repeat. Pay attention to people and how they feel. Be well meaning, well intended, be a team player. And then, go out and get drunk with them, or whatever they do that provides the equivalent loss of control.

Other than paying attention to people, common sense, an observant nature, a few hours of research, I wouldn't do anything else before starting to work in a new culture. I'm not saying I would get to know a culture so quickly, I am saying I would know enough to start, and start learning more. Good intentions, clear, transmitter accountable communication style, a healthy dose of humbleness, self confidence and contextual awareness are a good enough start for any culture.

When people and teams fail due to cultural differences, they rarely fail because of lack of information on the finer points of the other's history or obscure social habits. They fail because of assumptions that are never tested and because of people that don't put in the work to sense a room, to test a position, to ask the right questions, to push for clarity. They fail because of a lack of Compassionate Radical Honesty. Sure, they can also fail because they're assholes, but let's work with the assumption of well intended people.

When I first worked with brits, for months, I would join conference calls, would talk for an hour, opinions would be exchanged, but half the time I couldn't understand when a decision was made and, if it was, what was it. We could do this, we might do that, why don't we try that. It seemed like the whole conversation was like that, an endless enumeration of meandering possibilities, and then at some point, it would suddenly end. Nobody would say, "ok, so the decision is X and I'd like Michael to do it" or anything that remotely sounded like a conclusion, but they would all seem happy with the situation. I immediately realized my difficulty in understanding what was being agreed so I started applying compensatory measures: I would pay extra attention. I would double check. I would ask. I would probe what others understood. I would learn. I would get better at picking up cues, rhythms and nuances. I would give them feedback in how to help us, typical Romanians, understand better what they wanted. In a few months, I got pretty good at understanding their communication style and I helped others understand it as well. All it took was the self awareness to realize I had a problem, and some common sense measures to compensate for it and fix it.

I also remember a conversation I've had with an American senior manager that would occasionally come here to talk about plans and products, to rally the troops. In his all-hands meetings, he would never get more than polite but silent attention and maybe, if he was lucky, a couple of questions. He didn't understand what he did wrong. Worried and concerned, he asked me, why wasn't he getting through? I told him that is as good as it gets! Romanians don't smile a lot, don't clap too much and definitely don't cheer. Silent attention was how it looked when it was good. Say your thing and then probe with individuals later on. Test your impact. Test your message.

Death by politeness

On August 6th 1997, at night and in bad weather, flight Korean Airlines 801, an Airbus A300, was getting ready land in Guam. It was carrying 254 people, a cockpit crew of three and it had something else on board as well, something that proved fatal: a culture of deference and obedience. As they were maneuvering to land, the tired captain made mistake after mistake, while the first officer and the flight engineer, who had a better grasp of the situation, only dared hint at the problem. Several times they said that the airport is not in sight, when it should have been. Procedure was clear: if the airport is not visible by a certain altitude, the landing is to be aborted immediately, but nobody spoke up boldly and clearly, and they continued. They expressed their concern as respectful suggestions, words left to float around, for the captain to pick them up and decide what to do with them. He didn't do anything. "*The glide scope is incorrect*" said another crew member, to no reaction. A minute later the captain asks "*Isn't the glide slope working?*". They see nothing in the stormy night, they have no visuals, and they are not aligned to the radio beacons, and yet, still, they keep descending as if everything is ok. The computer reads out the altitude. 1000 feet. 500 feet. They lower the landing gear, getting ready for touchdown, still going as if everything was on track. It was 12 seconds before impact, when the ground proximity system started blaring out, that the first office finally said what he wanted to say for minutes, but never dared: he declared a missed approach. The captain finally reacted and pulled up. It was too late. The crash happened so unexpectedly, said Hyun Seong Hong, one of the 26 survivors, that passengers "*had no time to scream*". The crew on the other hand had all the time in the world and dozens of chances to simply pull back and go around, but didn't.

I first saw this as a teenager, on one of the Air Crash Investigation episodes. I couldn't understand how a perfectly functioning aircraft and a highly trained crew of three could knowingly fly straight into a mountain, towards their death, because nobody said something clear before it was too late. How can you die out of too much politeness? The copilot and the flight engineer knew. They knew!

Today, I don't have any more problems understanding it. Fortunately, I've never witnessed an aircraft flying into a mountain, but I've seen too many projects and teams crashing and burning for the exact same reason. These teams too were in perfect flying condition, just like the Korean Air plane: they were made up of skilled individuals, well intended, equipped with the resources and tools they required to get the job done. They had all they needed to detect the mountain they were hurling towards and to say something about it, but they didn't. When you talk to a project team post mortem, after a big project crash, trying to understand what happened, how did it fail so badly and so unexpectedly, they all tend to act like they knew it was coming, and I don't think it's just hindsight bias. It was obvious they say. When you ask them why they didn't do something, why didn't they say something, most will immediately protest: "I did!", followed by "But I wasn't heard". Go to the leader and they'll say that yeah, there was grumbling, but no risk was ever clearly raised. What a clusterfuck.

Before I go further, just want to be clear that I am not trying to dilute responsibility: final accountability always rests with the leader. However, that having been said, as the air travel industry painfully learned, it is not enough to rely on a single individual to be the only one that is able and expected to make clear, bold decisions in the face of changing circumstances. That individual, no matter how good or motivated, will eventually fail and, if there's nobody around to properly challenge him, he will bring down the whole team. You need everyone to be in a mindset where they each own, as much as they can, the success of the entire project. They need to speak up boldly and clearly, they need to speak up even when the captain is not speaking up, and if the captain doesn't seem to understand what they're saying, they need to make themselves understood. The set of principles and practices the airline industry developed and improved in the wake of Korean 801 and other fatal crashes caused by poor crew communication is called CRM, or Crew Resource Management: *"The term "cockpit resource management" (later generalized to "crew resource management") was coined in 1979 by NASA psychologist John Lauber who had studied communication processes in cockpits for several years. While retaining a command hierarchy, the concept was intended to foster a less authoritarian cockpit culture, where co-pilots were encouraged to question captains if they observed them making mistakes"*. CRM would be surprisingly familiar to us: it talks about assertiveness, active listening, proactivity. I will focus on something even simpler, one concept, just one idea to remember, internalize and apply at all times: communication accountability.

The key question is: are you responsible to make yourself understood or is whoever you're talking to responsible to understand you? If you lean towards the first, you have what is called transmitter accountability. If you lean towards the latter, you have what is called receiver accountability.

In transmitter accountability cultures, people work with the assumption that it's on them to make themselves understood. If they are not understood at first, they need to repeat the message. If they are still not understood, they will rephrase. If they are still not understood, they will try again, in a more serious tone. If they still can't get through, they will ask for help. In a transmitter accountability culture, "I said it, but I was not understood" can not be and is never a valid excuse. Speaking without making yourself understood is about as useful as not even trying.

Receiver accountability cultures on other hand, work with the assumption that we say things and those listening will decide if they want to hear, understand, ask for more information, do something with it, or not. Once you've said it, your job is done. Now it's up to them to probe for more if they choose to. "I said it, but I was not understood" is a perfectly valid excuse in receiver accountability cultures.

Transmitter accountability cultures tend to use direct, clear and unambiguous messages. Things are said plainly, completely, acknowledgment is asked from the other party. Receiver accountability cultures soften the message and send out hints and suggestions. Transmitter accountability cultures are egalitarian, while receiver accountability cultures consider that saying things too bluntly in front of your seniors is a sign of serious disrespect, a lack of sophistication and elegance. You're supposed to hint at the problem, almost embarrassed that you're even bringing it up, and let them figure out the implied, but not stated, meaning behind it. *"Today the weather radar has helped us a lot"*, said the Korean 801 first officer, hinting towards the captain that the visibility was bad, and the situation complicated. *"Yes, they are very useful"*, replied the captain. Culturally, he was expected to pick up on the hidden message, on the meaning behind the words, and start asking questions, making decisions. That day he didn't.

My advice is clear: national culture aside, in business, choose transmitter accountability. Starting today, take ownership of your communication: you are responsible to make yourself understood. "I said it but they didn't get it" is never going to be an excuse for you ever again.

And last but not least, you, as a leader, need to be able to do both. Be both able to pick up the subtlest hints and also able to express yourself with absolute clarity. As cultural and operating tendency in your company however, lean strongly towards transmitter accountability.

What transparency is and isn't

Transparency in business is, generally, a very good thing. It helps the culture, because everyone understands how the leaders think, what the operating principles are, what matters, where is the company going and why. Transparency is also good pragmatically, because people who have information at their convenient disposal tend to be better informed, make better decisions, connect dots, come up with innovative ideas, perform better. There's also an argument to be made that things, be it products, systems, processes, they are all made stronger through transparency, because they are exposed to a sort of continuous beta testing, flaws constantly identified, fixed.

However, too many managers confuse transparency with a data stream. By all means, have data streams, put spreadsheets with detailed numbers of every business parameter out there, make them available, searchable, usable, publish everything. A part of this is necessary for any kind of transparency, and if you want to do more than most, more power to you.

But that's not the most important part of transparency. The most important part of transparency, the one that really matters, is leadership transparency. Why do leaders act the way they act, what are they thinking, what are they prioritizing, what rulebook are they following, what culture are they building, what decisions are they making and why? This is the transparency that matters, the cultural transparency. Transparency is vulnerability because the leader who is honest exposes herself to potential criticism and makes it clear to all that she doesn't have all the answers. A big part of transparency is not only transmitting what is known, but also what is unknown. What are the big questions we're struggling with? What are the business dilemmas? What are the uncertainties?

In order to achieve this kind of transparency, it's not enough for leaders to not hide information. It is not enough for them to answer when asked. It is not enough to publish a report. Transparency is not a state, it's a process. Transparency is a constant communication effort. Leaders need to continuously take steps to ensure they are communicating what matters in a way that is understood and that is, almost always, more than pointing to data streams. Transparency is data, but it's so much more than data.

Compassion

The first person I had to fire was the hardest, not only because he was the first and not only because it was early in my career, but also because he was the sweetest guy. Always gentle, hard working, never hurt a fly, never bothered anyone. He just couldn't keep up, it was all too much for him, at that time, with what we were doing. We took it slowly, gave feedback that got slightly stronger every time we gave it, drafted performance improvement plans, the whole thing altogether took six months. I did what I had to do, but I felt bad at many steps of the way. I always wanted the best possible outcome for him. When it was reasonable to hope he could turn it around, I hoped. When there was no more hope, I wanted to end it as well as possible for him, mentally, financially, in any way. I genuinely believed he could find success in the industry, he just needed a different curve to climb and, from what I hear, I was proven right. It was before my Compassionate Radical Honesty days, but even now, I would do it similarly. Faster, wouldn't take so long, I would be blunter, skip some steps, but nothing fundamental would change: at every step of the way I would believe in him as much I reasonably could, and I would help with anything I could. I would not hesitate to do what I have to do to protect the performance of the team and the business, but, at the same time, I would go out of my way to try to eke out, even in a difficult situation such as this, the outcome that would come closest to what could possibly be described as a win-win.

I always try to help the other guy get a win too, come out of the situation well, especially with people that weren't persistent assholes. I could be a saint, and at times I've been one, but I don't want to make a habit out of it. If you're mean to me on purpose, repeatedly, gratuitously, and I think you know what you're doing, well, I won't respond in kind, but my compassion for you will be at a cold minimum. I go to great lengths to not confuse weakness with malice. It's easy to see enemies everywhere and imagine vile intentions, but reality tends to be much more prosaic, fuller with stumbling, clumsy people than archvillains. True malice is extremely rare. Vast majority of people will wake up in the morning looking in the mirror thinking they're the good guys. If you're being mean out of weakness, that's one thing, one response from me. If you're being mean out of malice, that's a different response. I think I've met only a couple of true sociopaths in my business career so far, but I've met hundreds of people that insulted and hurt their colleagues because they were driven by their own fears and stupidities. We all did it, we all do it, it's human. We work really hard at it, and, with the Mental Sherlock and with a lot of practice, we get better at it, and we do it less and less. We get more self confident, we know what matters to us, we know what we stand for, and we get more accepting and more forgiving of mistakes. We get more compassionate. Not weak, not indecisive, compassionate. The stronger we get, the more confidence we have, the more compassionate we are.

I for one have this justice drive and, combined with my instinctive rejection of authority, I find it much easier to be tough with people in position of power than with those that are not. The more I think you can take it, the more I will ask from you, the blunter my feedback will be. I am not bothered by powerful people attacking each other in business. When you choose to play the game, then you're playing the game, and the business game, when played to the end, is not, generally speaking, a friendship game. You expect solidarity from your team, but you can't expect the same solidarity from all clients, partners, competitors, lawyers and what not. Some people will come at you hard, and that's ok, because that's the game. I meet all people with no expectations, I keep my mind clear. I don't expect them to be mean to me, I don't expect them to want to cheat me, and I don't expect them to be my friends or to want to help me. Statistically, I expect them to be what most people are, trying to get by, do what they like, follow their interests and be polite. However, I don't hold these expectations dear, they're not emotional expectations, they're just statistics. This detachment allows me to better see people for what they are, with all their strengths and weaknesses. And, if it so happens that they are going to be my adversaries in some initiative or another, or behave in a certain way, I am not disappointed. I can not be disappointed by people I have no expectations of and I have no expectations from strangers or random acquaintances. I have expectations from my team, I have expectations from my partners. Anyone else doesn't owe me anything and I don't take anything for granted. When I get really upset is when people in power are mean to people with far less power. People that are not trying to be the next CEO, that are not dealmakers, not trying to get that big job, not playing politics, these are civilians, trying to do as good of a job as they can, get through the day, leave something behind, go home in the evening and spend time with their families. I hate it when people are mean to civilians.

Don't get me wrong. I don't think myopically hypercompetitive cultures are good. All I'm saying is that if intentional aggression is allowed at all, it should only be allowed among players, and never on civilians. I still think that, inside the company, you should always aim for a culture, aggressive or not, where all employees, at all levels, can count on each other and trust each other. All conflict, if there is, and there should be, is positive, idea based conflict, not petty, not a power game. All internal competitiveness, if there is, should be collegial. However, as you get to be more senior, your circle of business interactions will extend outside your company, with partners, suppliers, clients. Extend your best intentions to everyone, be honest, be truthful, be forthcoming, be good, but don't take anything for granted. They don't yet owe you anything. You may develop trusted relationships with some of them, but you haven't yet, and with some you never will. They're not your friends, and I don't mean to say this with sadness, or cynicism. They just aren't, they are something else.

To complicate things more, the "company" is a fluid entity. Large companies are frequently balkanized, and loyalty and trust is usually given to the immediate center, department or business unit more than to the company as a whole. Different sections of the company can sometimes be meaner to each other than to competitors, a sad but frequent state of affairs in badly run corporations. Companies also use many contractors and suppliers these days and while you can definitely expect professionalism from them, you can't, by default at least, expect the same adherence to the culture as you would expect from a fellow employee. I for one am always an advocate of generosity and big thinking. Extend your best intentions and your best expectations to everyone, don't be tribal. Be ready to sometimes not be reciprocated, deal with it, don't get bitter and cynical. Cynicism is, more often than not, a defense mechanism coming out of weakness. If we think everyone is an asshole, then we can not be disappointed, that's the thinking behind cynicism, and it's weakness. I prefer the stoic way of not having expectations, as I described above. I don't clear my mind of expectations because of fear of failure or betrayal, but for clarity of mind, because expectations cloud judgement and can function as another form of unwanted bias. The stoic attitude towards expectations is a positive, constructive, and ultimately, a generous and compassionate attitude.

The bottom line I'm getting to is that compassion is more complicated than it seems. You have a basic level of compassion you show to anyone. This is your baseline, your default decency. Excepted from this are the true sociopaths, those that repeatedly attack you or others knowingly and for no justifiable reason, to which you show minimum compassion. Be careful to not see enemies everywhere though, they are rarer than you might fear; most people are just stumbling along doing their own thing and they're stepping on your toes not because of you, but because they're just people.

You have a higher level of compassion you show to people that you work with, or who have also shown compassion to you too. Colleagues, partners.

The highest level of compassion, the complete trust, is what you have for your core team, your brothers and sisters at work.

How you define these circles, how tribal you are, how you see your tribe, how generous you are in extending your compassion outside an inner circle, this will define you as a leader. I for one do not want to be a leader of a faction, so I try to extend my compassion with all the generosity I am capable of. You make your own choice.

On a power scale, you should be more compassionate to the weaker and the innocent. The strong and powerful also need compassion, they are human, but they can take a bigger portion of tough love. There's no excuse however for being mean to those that can't defend themselves. If I see you doing that, you're on my bad side.

When and how to apologize

You will make mistakes and you will offend, upset and disappointed people. Hopefully this isn't going to be the majority of what you do, but, if you want to get anything real done, you will do this as well and there's no way around it. The only people that don't ever cause any trouble are the people not trying to do anything of consequence.

There's more than one way to upset and offend people and each requires a different reaction.

Your ideal is to constantly challenge and push everyone around you towards a better way of doing things, by offering Compassionate

Radical Honesty. You will do this in a way that is obviously for the greater good, not for your own interest, you will do it in a moral way and you will also be about getting the best out of the situation and out of everyone, about empowering and progressing, not about belittling individuals. Even if you manage to be this ideal leader, and you won't, not all the time, but even assuming that you do, people will still snap around you. They may feel pushed too hard, they may feel unappreciated or they may just be going through a phase, doesn't even matter. You need to show compassion, you need to encourage, you need to help, you need to have patience, but you don't need to apologize. You didn't do anything wrong, you just kept a high standard. Yes, maybe you pushed too hard, admit that, but don't apologize. Admitting a mistake, lending a helping hand, revising a decision, changing course, these are not the same as an apology.

Sometimes, on the other hand, you will lose control and react in an over emotional way. For example, you may unload some very intense negative feedback on someone, way beyond what would be required to convey the message. If you do that, you need to apologize. If you were right in the core of your feedback, then double down on the key message, stick to it, but apologize for giving it in an unprofessional way. Stick to the idea, apologize for the delivery. If you did it in private, apologize in private. If you did it in public, apologize in public. Don't overdo it, not for every slight overreaction you might have, but do it when you really mess up.

Sometimes, you may be sorry about something. Maybe you insisted on a course of action, despite the feedback of your team, and that course of action didn't lead to the expected results. Expressing regret and apologizing are two different things. Saying you're sorry something happened the way it happened is not the same as an apology, it's simply a sign of emotional and cognitive maturity and shows your ability to learn. Apologize only if you were unreasonable, if you irrationally discounted your team's feedback. If you were however rational and logical in your actions, to the best of what you could know at that time, there is no need to apologize. You may regret it, you may need to explain it better, you may decide to do it differently the next time, and tell them that, but you don't need to apologize.

It's ok to be vulnerable and apologize when you need, admit regret when you feel it, change course when it's the right thing to do, but don't overdo it. Apologizing too much is as bad as never apologizing.

Last but not least, check your ego. I am teaching you a fine line here, I'm telling you that you will inevitably upset some people and you just have to accept that. Be really careful that you do not go too far and end up turning into an egotistical boss, unnecessarily pushing people around, carelessly hurting people, and then just justifying it away as always being their problem, you always being the good guy doing the right thing and them being too touchy and sensitive. Always ask yourself, are you being tough because there is no other way and are you really doing it for the team, for the company, or do you do so it just because it's easy and you like it? The former is good, the latter is, in and by itself, not. With great power comes great responsibility.

The right kind of stubbornness

Once you employ CRH, you may find yourself speaking out more, taking more positions, asking more questions, criticizing things more vigorously, proposing more initiatives. It's an addictive feeling. CRH is however not a reason to lose sight of the strategic objective, of the priorities. The fact that you now can speak about anything doesn't mean that you should. You still need a sense of what matters now and what can wait. If you choose to speak out about everything all the time, you'll bog down every meeting you attend. You'll also need to remember that some decisions will have to be, in a sense, leaps of faith, due to the inherent uncertainty of the situation, and there's no way around it. Just because you know how to do something, doesn't mean that you need to do it all the time. Don't be Cartman, who was gratuitously being a pain in the neck to everyone about everything and, when challenged, would argue "What, I'm just asking questions!"

Earning the right

Compassionate Radical Honesty is about your behavior, but also about who you are to the people you're doing it with. If your team knows you, and trusts you, and knows you're always out to protect them and the common good and do good work, then it will be comparatively easy for you to engage in Compassionate Radical Honesty. Your messages will be perceived in the most positive possible light and even when you slip and sometimes don't explain something right or maybe even misuse some words, or go a bit too far, you will get the benefit of the doubt and they will tend to forgive.

If you're a new manager, you will need to be more careful. You will need to explain more and better and be more careful about your words. Explain what you're doing, repeat, validate, test, check. Explicitly tie your messages to the common problems, so the team knows you're doing it because you're trying to fix the important issues. Do use CRH as a new manager, but make sure you explain yourself well, so the team understands what you're saying, and more importantly, why you are saying it. They don't know you and don't yet visceral trust you, so make sure they know you're doing it for the right reasons. Leave no room for imagination, take extra steps to show you're only interested in the common good.

As you're being direct, as you're being honest, as you're making the tough decisions, as you're being confident, also be humble. Don't brag, don't let yourself fall prey to hubris, take it easy with the privileges your seniority may get you, don't jump the queue, be respectful, show integrity and humility.

Compassionate Radical Honesty is not an excuse for shallow arrogance or callousness. Earn your right to be radically honest.

Step 4: Get the right people

There are two sides to getting the right people. The first is building something worth joining and being someone worth following and a lot of this book is about that. This chapter is specifically about attracting and selecting them well, about how to know what you're looking for, how to distinguish between the real deal and the pretenders. Fewer things are more important in business.

Hire better

How do you select the right people for your team? What do you ask them, what do you look for, how do you decide?

There are two types of recruiting: internal, when you get someone from the same company but from outside your current team, and external, when you hire from outside the company. The differences are not as large as they might initially seem and most of the concerns and mechanisms are the same. I'll highlight the differences, but they are mostly of degree, not of nature.

The typical way in which a hiring process, internal or not, works, is the following:
1. You, the hiring party, put out a job ad, typically a piece of text, often the actual job description, signaling availability and inviting people to come and try for it. Alternatively, in talent constrained markets, you have to chase them and convince them to come to the interview. You typically do some of both.
2. They come to the interview and usually bring a resume, a history of their professional life. Starting from their resume and the job description, you ask questions and engage in dialogue, to determine their skills, attitude, fit for the job and also, at the same time, to answer their questions and help them understand who you are and why they should join you. Sometime before or after the interview you may also get references about the candidate, so you get to hear from a trusted source of how they performed in other places.

3. You decide if you want them, and if you do, you make them an offer, which they decide to accept, reject, or negotiate.

The process is standardizable and scalable. Job descriptions provide a canon version of what you're looking for. More recruiters can be hired to contact more candidates and the process can be automated and optimized. Job ads can be put out and advertised, to attract more people. You can put KPI's on this process and measure all kinds of things, such as reach of your ads, number of resumes received, number of interviews etc. It's a corporate dream, a machine that mediocre managers can do a mediocre job of running.

Let's talk about all the ways in which it can fail and all the ways in which you can make it great.

It starts with understanding who you are, as a company, as a team, as a leader. What do you really need, what do you really want, what is it that you're actually looking for? It is so easy to fool ourselves and imagine we're something other than we really are. Some teams and companies don't even try to answer this anymore, they just run with the template, throw in everything and the kitchen sink when it comes to required skills, ask for the same clichés of "work hard play hard" or any of countless similar platitudes floating around, and end it with a plastic looking, fake sounding description of the company. We all want, or think we want, the best people, but the best at what? Also, are we willing to pay for the best, in salary, but also, more subtly, and more importantly, in care and attention afterwards? The best people need great opportunities, expect a certain kind of treatment, come with certain expectations. Do we really know what they need and are we ready to give it to them? You want to attract special people, but what is it special about you as a leader and as a company? Don't rush into a generic kitchen job ad, spend the time for introspection, to understand who you really are and what you're looking for, and, whatever you do, don't fall back to the easy way out, the "funny" job ad, as a way to hide your confusion. Think hard, make some choices, and put the truth into what you're going to say. It's not meant to entertain, it's meant to communicate what matters.

It continues with marketing and by that I mean good marketing. The job you're offering is a product and just like any good product, it should communicate some very clear things about it and, through that, attract a certain kind of client, or, in our case, candidate. What you never want to do is sell a washing machine: they all look the same, do the same, and nobody cares about anything but which one is the cheapest or, in our case, pays the most. The candidate's disinterest for your "values" or whatever you think makes you unique and interesting starts with you doing a bad job of communicating that as part of your hiring process, and not being authentic and believable. Your corporate looking job ad is a boring job description, clumsily prefaced by some funny sentences or a couple of hashtags, designed to make you look cooler, but only succeeding in making you look like grandpa trying to rap. At the other extreme of the spectrum, but equally uninspiring, you have the startup where every job title contains the word "ninja" in it and the list of responsibilities includes "making the world a better place". None of this, while marginally useful as rough information, tells your audience what the authentic personality of your team is and what are you really looking for. Do you want interesting people to want to work with you? Then be interesting. Do you have an inspiring CEO? Are you working in one of the companies where the rockstar founder is still around and that in itself is a brand? Use that. Have you personally ever stepped out of your office and spoken at a conference or mingled at a meetup, gave people a chance to know you and see what you care about? Does anyone know who you are or is your company hiring generic professionals to work for generic managers and, in this case, the generic manager happens to be you? Just another software developer coming at company X to work for just another engineering manager, on just another project. You need to make yourself known and you need to tell an authentic, compelling story about who you are and what you're looking for. The risk you run with this is that when you say something real about yourself, when you take some clear stand, you will discourage a certain part of the potential candidates and this is the kind of risk mediocre managers don't know how to take, because they don't understand that in order to generate some real interest you've got to stand for something. Trying to be a little bit of everything for everyone means you're nothing, for nobody. You're just another washing machine and you better hope you're the cheapest or closest to the door or something, because that will be the only reason people will choose you.

When Valve's employee handbook started making the rounds, describing the very unusual, very flat and decentralized management system they had, that was marketing gold for them as an employer. There were people here in Iași, half a planet away, drooling about working for Valve, and what they were drooling about was only partially the specifics described in that document. As attractive as what they actually said might have been, or maybe even more attractive, was that they boldly stood for something clear, something they believed in, and in that they were the polar opposite of the typical boring company trying very hard to say nothing and upset no one. It was even better that it was not a hiring ad, it was the actual employee handbook, in use internally, it was an actual thing, not just a marketing artifact.

When Elon Musk tweets about spending up to 3 days in a row in the Tesla factory, working 20 hour days, sleeping on a mattress, he is instantly pushing away any prospective candidate looking for work-life balance and at the same time attracting those looking for the highest intensity and highest profile job they can get. You and I are not Elon, but what's stopping us from going to the local industry conference and saying something equally clear about who we are, how we work and what we do?

What is the problem you're solving? Maybe your company is small, maybe your office unassuming, maybe you don't have a lot of money, but you're passionate about what you're doing. What are you doing? Where are you going? What drives you?

Stand for something, be authentic and if you manage to do that you might get interesting candidates and not just cookie cutter job seekers.

Next comes the interview. The point of the interview is to establish soul to soul connection and by this I don't mean intrusive, unnecessarily personal discussions, I mean that you need to understand what drives them and why they're there, and they need to understand what drives you and why you might want them to join your team. In the way of getting to this kind of real connection is everything else: canned questions, fear of failure, lack of real motivation, a scripted interview process with overly detailed forms to fill in and checklists to check. Instead of all that, sit down, ask open ended questions and let them speak. Listen, interject rarely, to ask for more details, to ask for clarification. Make them dive right into the core of an issue. "We delivered the project on time" means nothing. What project? What was difficult about it? Who did what in the team? What did they personally do? Were they a key player? How did they change during this project? Did they learn anything new? What do they think about their team mates? About the client? What would they do differently the next time? Your aim is not to ask questions, but to have a conversation, albeit an asymmetrical one, where the candidate does 80% of the talking. Ask them outright, what do they want? Use these words, ask them what they want. What are they looking for? What are they missing in their current job? What would make the difference? Tell them what you expect. What will be hard and unusual about working in your team? Talk about the future as you see it, about your ambitions, about how you like to work, about the other team members. Be confident, let promising candidates meet the whole team, let them wander around the office, unaccompanied even. In brief, focus on what they did, what they really did, dig deep, understand who they really are, and from your side, show yourself as you are.

The open secret. You probably know who you want to work with and who you don't want to work within the first 20 minutes of the interview. Hell, maybe in the first 5. All you're doing after that is just making sure you weren't seduced by some halo effect first impressions. Take the time to make sure a candidate you initially thought was great is indeed great, but don't take the time to make a candidate you initially found bad grow in your eyes. If you don't want to work with them, you don't want to work with them, it's not even about how good or bad they are. Don't fool yourself that you'll grow into it, you won't. If you are a mature leader, you will make this kind of instinctive decisions based on the right things, you won't select people that flatter you or people that play to your biases, but you will select talent, drive and that something special that you want in your team. If you are superficial, you will surround yourself with useless ass kissers.

Don't select for lack of weaknesses, select for strength. If you have a checklist and you tick every box they check and then you count the number of boxes ticked, you're going to end up hiring well rounded mediocrity, people that have a bit of this and a bit of that. What you want is real strength. Get that kick ass developer that can do in one night what others do in a month, even if he doesn't like to talk to anyone. Get that sales guy that can sell refrigerators to Eskimos, even if she doesn't have the patience to listen to the long presentations the tech team does for her. Yes, some level of teamwork and common purpose is required, and outright destructive behavior is never ok, but at the end of the day, better to have some difficult superstars than a team full of easy going averages. Pay special attention to reliability however. Even difficult superstars have to be reliable, if in nothing else, then in their key skill. That amazing salesperson might not be reliable when it comes to filling in her timesheets, but she better be reliable when it comes to selling. Throw away the checklist or use it simply as a kind of note taking. Hire people that shine brightly in some things, not only Even Stevens that do a little of this and a little of that, jacks of all trades, masters of none. I've hired for strength plenty of times and it didn't always work out, but it mostly did, and I never regretted it. What I got out of taking chances like these was way more than what I lost when I occasionally got it wrong, and, more importantly, way more than what I would have gotten from a bland, corporate, safe approach.

One person makes the decision. Committee hiring, like any other committee decision, drifts to the average and to the safety of mediocrity. Many can see the candidate, and more than one should, many can weigh in with an opinion, but only one makes the hiring decision.

Protect the culture. You can take a lot of chances with hiring. You can hire difficult people, you can hire stubborn people, you can hire overly confident people, even bordering on arrogance, but what you can not hire is those people that will wreck your culture. Avoid them like the plague, no matter how good they are. Reject politicians. Reject dishonesty. Reject meanness. Reject bullies.

Experience vs potential. Each has its value and there will be situations where you will be forced to value one or the other more. If you need immediate productivity, you hire experience. My personal bias has always been for potential, raw talent. I see the good side of experience, but I also see the bad side: fixed mindset, a decreased appetite for the new, rigid thinking. I balance both, but I lean towards potential.

With great power, comes great responsibility. I put a lot of emphasis on your freedom and right, as a leader, to pick your team on subjective reasons and on personal compatibility. I do not think you should be constrained by checklists or scorecards, I think you should make the hiring decision. With this kind of freedom, you could easily become a superficial, discriminating, unethical, egotistical manager. Develop your Mental Sherlock, stay true to yourself, think of the bigger purpose, be firm but generous, put the team before your needs and you will end up making good hiring decisions that you can be proud of.

All in all, when you decide what's most important to you, there are only two hiring questions you need to answer:
1. Do you need someone to hit the ground running on day one, or can you take a chance and invest in potential?
2. Do you want to put together the best possible team, or are you engaged in statistical hiring?

The first question will determine if you hire for potential or for experience. Do you go with a known quantity, or can you take a chance on something riskier, but potentially better?

The second question will determine how fanatical you need to be. In your startup, or in some elite team, you will obsess about getting the absolute best you can, whatever best means for you. If, on the other hand, you're in charge of staffing a division of hundreds inside a company of thousands, you understand you're playing a numbers game. You may still have high standards, but you know you need to focus more on your key players and that, out of those hundreds, a percentage will fail, will slip through, will be mediocre or worse. What you will then need, alongside your hiring process, is a scalable performance process to know how everyone is doing and to act on it.

Advanced intuition

Long time ago, we had a guy at an interview for a programmer job and he was ok technically, and ok technically was hard to get and we really needed that, so there was a lot of temptation to hire. There were three of us in the room with him for the final interview. He was easy going, answered eagerly all our questions, showed flexibility and looked like he wanted to please. All was good on paper, nothing bad to say, he had the right skills, we had agreement on the money, we were ready to go. Only thing was that something just didn't feel right. We didn't know how to put it in words, but we had this nagging feeling, he just felt weird, and not the right kind of weird, so we started asking around at his former workplaces in a deeper way than we would usually do. We found out he had been fired, two months back, for sexual harassment. Not only that he had lied to us about still being employed there, but back in the early-ish 2000's, in a small company in Romania, sexual harassment was not a thing people obsessed about, so I don't know what he exactly did to get fired, but I am sure he did way worse than make an inappropriate joke at the wrong time. We turned him down and he then proceeded to harass me personally, for more than a year, with the occasional text and Facebook message, sometimes delirious, sometimes almost threatening, until he stopped. I don't know what became of him.

About that time, we had another guy interviewing with us. He came to the interview, suffering from a cold, dressed like crap, answering our questions curtly, with limited experience in IT, having just come back from a period abroad, where he had done something else. Maybe also helped by his fever, he seemed to not care that much if we wanted him or not, and he didn't hide it. He wasn't outright arrogant or offensive, he just didn't seem to give a damn which way it would go. Also following intuition, we decided to hire him, because we saw something in there that was interesting, and he showed potential. He stayed with us for many years and he became one of our best delivery people, a stellar example when it comes to dedication and drive. He had many flaws, some big, but what he was good at, he was really good at.

In both these cases, and many others, I followed my intuition. On paper, we shouldn't have hired the second guy and we should have hired the first. Thankfully, we did the opposite. Intuition is, in the modern work environment, harder and harder to follow. In big bureaucracies, intuitive decisions of all kinds, hiring among them, are hard to make and defend, so you've got to cover your intuition with the right kind of procedural crap to fool the process cops. Intuition can also be perceived as discriminatory. Following it can even open you to lawsuits. It's always easier, more trouble free, to just follow the process, fill in the interview report, say only what you're sure of, tick off the boxes, move on, but that means you don't give a damn, and if you don't care, you're not a leader.

I am a big fan of intuition, I think we need more of it, but what I call advanced intuition: give chances to people that wouldn't otherwise get a chance, if your intuition tells you there's something there; it's ok to make mistakes this way. On the other hand, when your intuition tells you to reject someone, be more careful: follow it, investigate, inform yourself. I've rejected people on intuition alone, with no more proof than that, but not many.

For clarity, intuition and cultural compatibility are not the same. When you reject someone for example because they are very rigid in thinking and you're looking for the opposite, that is not following your intuition, that is making an informed decision based on a soft skill, on an attitude that you can clearly see during the interview and also get references about. An intuitive decision is when you have to decide based on what you can not see, but can only sense.

Promote better

We all know about the Peter principle, which states that people get promoted until they reach their point of incompetence, and that's where they stay. You promote the good junior developer to be a senior developer and you promote the good senior developer to be a team leader. If she turns out to be a mediocre team leader, she will stay there, keep being mediocre, and you've just lost a good senior developer and gained a bad team leader.

Counter the Peter principle through your leadership culture. Don't make promotions look like a must have, as the only alternative to stagnation. Instead, let people keep doing a great job, the same great job, for a long time, and value them for that. When you do promote, make sure you promote based on the skill required in the new job, not based on performance in the current job. Sure, promotion is always partially a reward, so some kind of good performance in the current job is required, but that's not the point I'm making. What I am saying is that when you want to promote the good senior developer, make sure both she and you understand what the new job, team leader, is all about, and if it's the job she wants and in which she will continue to be successful. Being a good senior developer earned her the right to be considered, but she's not obligated to take it, and you're not obligated to give it. It may very well be that your next best team leader is not your current best senior developer, and it may also be that, for example, if your current best senior developer is really good, she'll be paid better than the team leader.

There are two ways to promote: you can stretch-promote, or you can promote the obvious. You stretch-promote when you put people in positions they and you are not sure they will handle, but you're taking the chance, and you're providing the right structure and coaching to guide them. You promote the obvious when you recognize that a person is mostly already acting at the next level and are largely already doing the new job. Both methods have their pros and cons, but decide what you want, and communicate it. Your people should know what kind of performance culture you have and when and how to expect promotions. I personally promote the obvious most of the times, but I do like a stretch promotion once in a while, as a way of trying something new, or giving someone a chance.

Loud culture vs quiet culture. Do you expect your people to come to you and ask for promotions, or do you expect them to quietly do a good job and wait to be offered one? Whichever you may want it to be, the main point is the same as above: communicate it, make clear what you expect. I personally lean towards loud, people asking for it, in which case I will use Compassionate Radical Honesty to tell them how I feel about their readiness and what it will take for them to get it. If I do this however without making it clear to all that this is how I work, I will risk being unfair. I need to make it clear to all that this is what I expect.

Don't reward bad behavior. If they are motivated and driven as a senior developer, they will be motivated and engaged as a team leader. If they are detached and entitled as a senior developer, they will be detached and entitled as a team leader. Don't use promotions as a motivation tool in order to fix bad behavior. If you have demotivated people, motivate them first, make sure they still have the fire in them, and then give them a shot at that promotion, if they get to deserve it again. Don't reward bad behavior with a promotion, or with any reward for that matter. If someone is trying to squeeze a promotion out of you by pissing the bed in their current job, make it clear you will not stand for it and they first need to get better in order to keep their current job, never mind get any promotion. Don't hesitate if they're technically good, they usually are. Rewards shouldn't be given to capable people with a bad attitude any more than they should be given to incompetents with good attitude.

As people do one thing, they do everything. This is a bit more controversial and I myself don't follow it to the letter, as I understand it can be ground for a whole bunch of unproductive biases, but I do keep it in the back of my mind. My intuition is this: as people do one thing in their life, they do everything in their life. If you go play tennis with two colleagues, and one comes all dressed up with specific gear, racket carefully packed, and takes 20 minutes to get ready, carefully taking everything out, warming up, and the other comes in shorts and snickers and just wants to have a go at it, that tells me something about how they're going to be at work too. Like I was saying, it's very easy to oversimplify and misuse this, so you've been warned.

Resist the easy option. Maybe one of your managers has left and her second in command is there, eager and apparently able to take her place. It's such an appealing choice, because he's there, you don't need to hire, you can fill the gap right now and move on, problem solved. Resist the easy option. The person you already have may indeed be the best choice, but make sure they are, because sometimes they're not. Competent lieutenants as they may have been up until now, this is something else. Don't do it just because it's convenient. If you need to, wait. If you need to disappoint someone, then so be it. What matters most is the health and performance of the team and that's your number one priority.

Fire better

Firing better usually means firing faster. It's as simple as this, somewhat ruthless, statement. 95% of the mistakes managers make with firing is not taking action soon enough. For reasons discussed all throughout this book, they avoid conflict, they postpone, they tolerate, they get stuck. Unsurprisingly, when they finally muster the courage to do it, or are forced to, the same fear of conflict makes them do it badly, by watering down the message and denying the person in question any real feedback, or from the contrary, scared out of their wits about what they have to do, they lose control and have the situation blow up in their face. Own it, do it, get it done.

Firing quickly is especially important if you want to be able to take chances during hiring, and sometimes you do, because you want to try new things. But how can you take hiring chances if, when you inevitably get it wrong, sooner or later, you can't efficiently fix your mistake?

Of course, you never want to play with people and you shouldn't hire someone on a whim, knowing that there's a 50% chance they won't make it through the first month, unless this is clear to them as well. But, even with a reasonably conservative hiring process, there will be a percentage of failures and you will need to deal with them.

You hope you won't have to get to firing, but you will, and when you get to it, do it fast. Don't linger.

Firing is not a power trip. It's not about shaming. It's not about punishing. It's about your team and who should be in it and who shouldn't. Be decent and do all you can to protect their dignity, their chances in the labor market, and their financial security, by offering severance if you can afford it. I am not talking about major assholes, disciplinary firings, or law breakers, I am talking about decent, hardworking people, that just couldn't fit in or couldn't cut it in your team, but that have a good chance of performing in other contexts. Treat them honestly, compassionately, and minimize their inevitable pain. You owe them quick, honest and respectful action. Letting them hang around on a career path to nowhere is not doing them a favor.

The first is going to be hard and then it will get easier.

Your reputation

Your reputation is the best kind of marketing you can have. You, personally, should be known in the industry, in your local circles, in your tech specialty, in your area of interest and people should know who you are. You can control your reputation through your speaking, your networking, your appearances, but your reputation is also made by what others are saying about you. It's better to have a reputation than not to have one, even as any reputation inevitably means that some parts of it will be bad, exaggerated or inaccurate, and that some people will speak untruths about you, some unwittingly, some deliberately. Even with that, as a leader, it's always better to have a reputation than to not have one. Find out what it is and build it further. Get out there in the community, speak, interact, make yourself known.

Useful networking

Inspired by something Casey Neistat said, about a year ago I implemented the following networking rule in my life: I will not meet with anyone, outside family, unless it's business or something I want to do. I am in a period in my life where I need focus and my business is diverse enough that I meet many kinds of people as part of normal work. Outside my direct business, I carefully choose the events I go to and when I go, I arrive late, I leave early, and I make sure I make the most out of them. If you ask me for a coffee to talk "about an idea", I will not come unless you tell me what the idea is and once you do that, 9 times out of 10, I will prefer to conclude the conversation right then and there, without the need for a meeting. By right then and there I usually mean text comms of some sort. I rarely if ever answer my phone when I don't have a previously agreed call and practically never to numbers I do not have in my agenda. If you want me, contact me by text or email and tell me clearly what you want. Don't ask me to invest a couple of hours by coming to talk about "an interesting opportunity", because unless you're either Elon, or my mother, I won't do it. I fully expect the same from you if I ask you to come and "hear an idea" from me.

Some years back I was doing the opposite. I was just starting to get involved in the community and I was interested in everything, I wanted to sample it all, so I said yes to everything, went everywhere and met almost anyone. I can't say I totally disliked it, but that was an exceptional situation. These days, I know what I want and what I need most is focus. I use events, such as conferences and meetups, to stay in touch with the new, but that's about it.

Step 5: Culture

What is culture

The most widely used definition of culture is that culture is the way we do things around here. I have a better one: culture is what happens when people care. Culture is the result of people giving a damn. Culture is not a set of polite norms and manners, culture is the result of personality applied onto work by people who care about more than doing "a job".

When, many years back, at my first real job as a software developer, at a company called Matrix, a few of us suddenly decided to spend 36 hours to throw away the couple of months of work on the product we were building and rewrite everything from scratch by first writing code generators and then write code that would fix classes of errors from the 7000 and something compilation errors we got on first pass, we didn't do this following a comprehensive cost-benefit analysis, we did it because it felt right, in that company, a startup of sorts before we even knew the word. It was a company where we, the 4-5 developers, would routinely code until 3 AM, and then the single tester would test between 3 and 5 AM, with us fixing bugs as she found them, after which the client implementation team, the owner and a couple of the developers, would start the 2 hour drive to our main client to deliver the new version on premise, at the start of their work day. In this kind of culture, our rewrite decision was the most natural thing to do, and we did it because we cared.

When I then started working for Synygy what struck me first was that, most people, and most of the key people, took their time to get it right, technically speaking. Debates could last for days on end about some detailed technical design issue that would have been a half an hour conversation in most places, or 30 seconds in Matrix. Slowing things down to get it right was the norm. Some team leads would even go as far as to say that tempering the enthusiasm of their people and helping them make more deliberate decisions was their most important job. A far cry from the move fast and break things approach at Matrix for sure, to borrow Zuckerberg's early Facebook mantra. A product company, Synygy did not have the client delivery pressure, and, a much larger company than Matrix, it had the financial comfort to take the time to ponder each and every technical decision. Another interesting thing about Synygy's slow down and get it right culture was that it was an unofficial culture. It didn't come down from the US based CEO and it wasn't written on the walls. It wasn't shared by the other delivery centers and even here in Iași there were some teams that, being connected more directly to managers elsewhere, were outside it. This culture was the personal style of a handful of key people here in Iași and, by being the first, they spread it, by hiring people with similar views and through their daily example. If anything, the local culture was a kind of protection against the larger company, against those managers from far away that, we thought, sometimes correctly, didn't understand what they were asking for or what good software was. That's how the thinking went anyway, and it was powerful. The CEO was far away, talking about things we didn't care about, there was no official culture to speak of, or at least one that I remember. They had the right to choose business priorities, but we worked our way, and it was going to be done when it was going to be done, and we were going to do it right and it was going to be right because we cared.

When, even later on, in my Endava experience, I would obsess about understanding the client's worldview and I would try to spread this obsession to my teams in every way I could, I didn't do it because I had just read a book or because I had a management objective about it, I did it because that company, a software services company, had a client first culture that was superbly exemplified by the CEO and the rest of the executive team. I resonated with it, it felt natural and the countless decisions, large and small, that we took to better deliver value to our clients came from that culture and from that culture alone, not from a direct instruction or a process or some other organizational imperative. In this kind of professional services environment with a consulting mindset, working closely with our large enterprise clients who wanted nothing more than predictability, on their complex mission critical systems, a decision like the one at Matrix, to just throw out two months' work on a whim and engage in some radical rewriting would have been unthinkable.

Culture is, yes, the way we do things around here, but that matters only when we care. Otherwise, culture is just a set of unwritten motions we go through. Culture starts being real, starts shaping things, starts being a multiplier of performance only when people give a damn, so do surround yourself with people that give a damn.

Why culture matters

Why do we even bother with culture? Why don't we just organize our companies carefully, put clear processes in place and just do things? What's all this culture thing about?

Two reasons why modern companies working in complex industries need strong and effective culture in order to be successful.

One, people. People need a purpose and commonly accepted codes of behavior that go towards making them feel like a team, a professional community, like they've got something more than just a paycheck. We will dive deeper into this in later chapters, but, simply put, people care about more than the mechanics of getting their job done. This is just human nature and without the right culture people aren't engaged, they suffer, and results suffer.

Two, complexity. In unpredictable knowledge industries you couldn't script the work of everyone in your team or company even if you wanted. You will have processes and guidelines, sure, but you could never develop the kind of detailed procedures that would tell your people exactly what to do in any situation and, if you tried, you would probably kill your business by suffocating all decision making. Instead, you need to accept that groups of people in your company, that you may not even personally know, will be faced with situations you can not foresee, and they will need to make important decisions in those undefined and ambiguous situations, decisions that you will never get a chance to review or even find out about, but that will affect the performance of your company. What is the best mechanism by which you increase the likelihood of such decision being the right decisions? Culture. Not the only one, but the best.

Your company culture is, yes, a people thing, as in it addresses job satisfaction and leads to engagement. It deals with the human aspect. It is however at the same time a pragmatic instrument for enabling good decisions, increasing performance, competitiveness and business success. For both these reasons, culture is not a "HR thing", or just an engagement tool, or something that you do out of the goodness of your heart because you're such a great boss. Culture is the CEO's job and final accountability for culture cannot be delegated down. In your team, in your area, where you are the leader, culture is your job, and although you will want and need to take everyone onboard with you and everybody needs to contribute, ultimate accountability rests firmly with you. Accountability for culture always trickles up to the most senior individual around.

Deterministic and free market

I will boil down all my experience and say that there are two main types of cultures and every culture is a mixture of them. In the end, the kind of culture you will want to have will be heavily constrained by two things: the kind of person you are, your natural inclination, and the hard constraints of the market in which you operate. Everything else is a choice you are free to make.

The first type of culture is deterministic. It is focused on the need to calculate and predict outcomes and then engage in deterministic plans to reach those outcomes. They use hierarchies to plan and push priorities, they use rules and standards to direct investment and control outcome.

The second type of culture is free market. It is focused on simple rules of interaction that allow actors to safely express themselves through value exchanges that can not be entirely foreseen or centralized, leading to unexpected results. They use appealing internal products, such as new initiatives and projects, to attract the attention of the internal market players, the employees, and the prevailing priorities and ethos are the result of the current market equilibrium, which is in constant flux.

A weird mix sometimes happens where a lot of free market like bets are made through the personal will of a strong CEO. Steve Jobs at Apple for example pushed through initiatives that were untested in the deterministic sense, there was no detailed research behind them, no pros and cons analysis, so major decision were made on personal will and intuition. In general, determinism is inversely proportional to the power of the CEO. A company with no single majority shareholder will tend to be deterministic, because determinism is much easier to sell to large groups of people who don't trust you. Results will have to be forecasted precisely and outcomes promised to shareholders, who are too many and too distributed to simply be convinced to go with a more unpredictable free market approach. Companies with a strong founder CEO on the other hand will usually be more free market, bolder and more experimental in their decisions. Google and later Alphabet burned through piles of cash on all kinds of experiments unrelated to their core business and with no immediate monetization potential, simply because Larry and Sergey could. When Steve Jobs ran with the 1984 ad, despite most of his board thinking it was going to be a disaster, he did it because he could. Jeff Bezos let third party sellers show up on amazon.com alongside its own offerings, letting customers choose the third parties if they had a better offer and losing money in the process, because he had a bigger vision of how that would end up making Amazon stronger in the end. No run of the mill Citicorp CEO will ever be able to do anything like that. He will have to justify every major decision in the averaging cost saving language of most corporations. Eccentricity, expressed as apparently outrageous ideas, is not going to work in that kind of environment.

Management, traditionally, as a practice, is deterministic. Managers, in their vanilla version, don't get to experiment, or to try things out, they get to plan, get buy in for their plans, carefully execute those plans and then justify their decisions through deterministic reports. That's not the kind of management I'm advocating for, although some of that discipline is required in any circumstance.

As companies move from generation one to generation two, from the founder to a hired CEO, they tend to move from free market to deterministic. If the powerful founder CEO had the authority to make big bets, the second generation has less of that power. The third, lesser even. Innovation slows down, bureaucracy flourishes, competitiveness is lost, stagnation ensues. The current great management experiment of Silicon Valley (not only, but that's where it started) is the attempt to keep companies forever young by forcing a perpetual bias towards free market thinking. Google does this through structure, through the way in which teams form, people move around, decisions are made. Apple did it through Jobs, who had the internal power to cut through any bureaucracy and do whatever he wanted to do, and he carefully handpicked a few others he gave some of that power to as well. When Bezos wrote his famous shareholder letter about always being day 1, startup, because *"day 2 is stasis. Followed by irrelevance. Followed by excruciating, painful decline. Followed by death. And that is why it is always Day 1"*, this is what he was talking about. Analyzing in detail what these and other companies are doing to keep their free market spirit would a book in itself, but in the simple possible way, I think they are maintaining and creating deliberate organizational ambiguity in order to force a kind of thinking and decision making that doesn't encourage routine and comfort. They're staying hungry by deliberately injecting a measure of chaos in their internal decision structure, while at the same time ruthlessly optimizing other processes and parts of the business. It will be interesting to see if they are able to keep this when moving to the next generation. Apple is the current big test. Microsoft lost it with the move from Gates to Ballmer. It's got some of it back now, but we'll have to see how much.

Professional monogamy

For the longest time, it was simple. If you were an employee of a company, then you worked for it and it alone, you were part of it, you represented it and you were full time employed there, typically aspiring at a long career inside it. The only socially accepted kind of work relationship was that of professional monogamy.

And, then, lines started to get blurred.

One way in which lines get blurred is through suppliers embedded in your operations, especially in service delivery. At Endava, we frequently used to have software development teams working alongside the client's software development teams, sometimes physically in the same location, in the client's office. Teams from other suppliers and individual contractors were also there, part of the same program, working on the same thing. It was nothing special to have routine project meetings where those around the table (and on the call) would be employed by 3 or 4 different entities. Our people there would be full time Endava employees, but surely, we, and the client expected them to adapt to the context, understand and take in the priorities, and, to some degree at least, adapt their communication style and professional habits to suit the culture of the client. Was the client company fond of ad hoc huddles and quick decisions? We would adapt to that. Were they a process oriented company, with a preference for thick and data rich slide decks formally presented to large audiences? Then we would do that. What was their dress code? While onsite, we would use it too. Neither us nor the client expected our people to fully get immersed in the client culture, after all, they were not part of the client inductions, training, performance management system or anything like that, but we would be expected to understand, adapt and adhere to the practical aspects of the client culture, in as much as it was necessary for the smooth and frictionless delivery of the work we were contracted to do. Lines would get further blurred in longer engagements. When we had people onsite for 6 months, or a year, working in the client office day in and day out, they would develop friendships, they would attend the client Christmas party, they would take part in all-hands meetings, they would become part of the office life there. Sometimes we lost these people as they became less and less Endava in all but contract, and more the client. Sometimes the client lost them, after having almost become part of the family, but the contract ended, and they had to come back home to be deployed on something else.

Companies also mix full time employees with individual contractors. Full time employees get training, have a career path, have 1-1s with their managers, get paid vacations and all the other things employees usually get it. They invest in the company, and the company invests in them and both sides are invested in their shared future. Sure, sometimes this is done well, sometimes not, but that's the general deal. Individual contractors on the other hand are paid at an hourly rate and they are experienced professionals the company expects to drop in and start delivering on day one. They get no training, they have no career path within the company, and their contract is usually limited to a particular project and can be terminated at any time if anything whatsoever changes. They have no long term investment in the company and the company has no long term investment in them. There are expectations of professional behavior on both sides, but no expectation of loyalty in the true sense of the word, no expectation of cultural adherence other than the adaptability and pragmatism that enables all good contractors to quickly get productive in all kinds of scenarios. What do you do if you are the manager of a team of 10, where 5 are your full time employees and 5 are contractors, and you are interested in creating a strong team culture? Do you do it with your employees and then you communicate the key expectations to the contractors, knowing they may do it out of professionalism but unlikely to really feel it? Probably, it's the reasonable thing to do. You could also try to treat your contractors just like employees, and that may work in some situations. You do the best you can, but the situation is definitely more complicated than only having full time employees.

But an even more transformative change is ongoing more recently. The situations above are, for better or worse, practical necessities. A more frontal cultural challenge to professional monogamy is happening at the moment, a principled one.

Professionals more and more demand flexibility in working time and location and want, or need, to be able to do commercial, paid work, alongside their main job. A very senior person in one of my teams asked, when we discussed his hiring for a full time top position, that he could continue to do occasional paid training and consulting work for other companies, sometimes other IT companies from Iași, that were also competing with us for the talent. I said yes, but that he should avoid doing it with our largest competitors and also that our work will take priority. He would take days off to do his training only if, on those days, there was nothing hurting in our company because of his absence.

I also know of developers that have an active social media presence, that are active at conferences, that have a deliberate personal/professional brand that they value, distinct and separated from that of their current employer, and intentionally so. When they join a company, in their mind, the company doesn't just want an employee, they want their brand and, on occasion, that's true. Sometimes, that makes them strong, sometimes that makes them fail at their job, because their attitude is one of "they hired me for who I am, and am I this and that and you take it or leave it", and that makes them less able to listen and adapt to the company culture, and generally listen to feedback and get better through it. Sometimes, the brand gets ahead of the real skill and the noise is stronger than what's behind it. Some other times, the brand is real and valuable, and companies indeed value it and hire the brand alongside the person, because their new employee's brand will help them attract more talent.

It's an interesting new world, but your responsibility as a leader remains the same: create a culture story that people can rally around and be part of, regardless of their employment relationship or their starting position in your professional relationships. A pinch of free market attitude will help you deal with the variance better. Too deterministic of an ambition may be a disadvantage in this context.

The official canon and the fan stories

Star Wars has a main storyline, which is what you see in the official movies. The story of Luke Skywalker, his father Anakin, Yoda, Obi Wan, more recently Rey, Kylo, Finn and the new generation. This official story line is called canon. It also has secondary storylines, like Rogue One, a movie made starting from a single sentence from the original trilogy's A New Hope, a mention in the intro saying that *"During the battle, rebel spies managed to steal secret plans to the Empire's ultimate weapon, the DEATH STAR"*. It's a sideline story, but it is still canon, because it too is an official movie. Canon means that it is official, it is sanctioned, and it has to be recognized in all of the Star

Wars lore, it can not be ignored. If Luke dies in the canon movies, then Luke is dead.

Alongside the canon, there are hundreds if not thousands of works that could be called fan fiction. From elaborate forum posts to speculation, short stories, full novels, unofficial fan made movies, short, long, good or bad, in which all kinds of things happen, sometimes contradicting each other, all written by fans, unofficially, without any involvement whatsoever from the official keepers of the Star Wars brand. These stories are surely part of what could be called the wider Star Wars culture, but they are not canon. They are not official. They are called the extended universe.

It's the same with your company culture. You need to get the canon right. What is the main storyline, what is happening there that everyone must adhere to? Alongside the canon, hundreds and thousands of little habits and routines will develop in teams, of all kinds. They too are culture. As long as they don't contradict or detract from the canon, they are beneficial and are the ways in which teams and group of people take the main story and make it their own, particularizing, extending it, taking it further. Don't fight fanfiction as long as it doesn't fight you. Celebrate the little habits and particular stories of specific teams and departments, but also highlight how they tie back into the main story, to the canon. You are celebrating them because they cared enough to find a way, unique to them, to contribute to the big story, in the area and way which is most the relevant to them. When the fanfiction starts to contradict or downplay the main story, then you need to quash it, but before that, look at your canon. Fan fiction tends to get destructive only when the canon is weak or being treated badly. Take good care of your canon and the fan fiction will naturally tend to be supportive and it will help rather than hinder.

Zombie culture is worse than no culture

Culture is an exercise in absolutist thinking. You will forgive people, you will understand situations, but you will never accept that the official canon of your culture is not ever burning with urgency. If it isn't, then you need to either rally your people, fire them if you can't, or change the culture, because something isn't working. Culture that is proclaimed to be important, but is routinely ignored in practice, is zombie culture, and is worse than no culture at all.

When it comes to culture and leadership principles there is no virtue in accommodating all sides and all points of view. You need to pick something and reject everything else, stand for something clear. Culture can't be introduced in a lukewarm fashion with an open ended deadline. "Guys, we should, in time, try to have a culture of radical honesty in our company so whenever you feel ready and comfortable, do try it, will you?" This is ridiculous and worse than not doing anything at all. Culture can only be discussed in terms of absolute imperative urgency. You will give people some time to understand the finer points, you will help them operationalize it, but any new culture item is always effective immediately and absolutely, no exceptions, no nuances. While you understand that the complete practical implementation of cultural imperatives may take some work and time, the ideological implementation should always be "starting now", because culture deals with such critical matters as trust, honesty, integrity, winning, compassion and things like this mean nothing if applied piecemeal or in steps. With culture, you are either in or out. I can accept that maybe you didn't realize you were breaking trust in a particular situation, and I will help you see that and correct it, through compassionate radical honesty, but I will never accept that trust itself is debatable or that we shouldn't always seek it. People fail, and we help each other overcome failure and weakness, but our values are our guiding light.

At the same time, and this apparent contradiction is one of the many contradictions leaders need to reconcile in their heads all the time, you know that some team somewhere under immense pressure to deliver may slip on the culture, and in this way, culture is a journey, not a destination. There's always some new employee that needs to be inducted but hasn't yet been exposed to all the nuances of your culture, there's always someone or another that needs help to stay on the straight and narrow and there may occasionally be someone that needs to go. Culture is never ending work and the moment you stop working on it is the moment it starts degrading and rotting. The moment you let something slip, your people will see it and they will magnify your mistake 10 times, 100 times, by each letting something slip too, and then their teams will let something slip, and soon enough nobody cares anymore. Culture, unlike other kinds of "resources", unlike skills, unlike money, unlike knowledge, is a very weird and capricious animal that you have to always be fanatical about or it will turn to dust faster than you can imagine.

Little Red Riding Hood and a safe culture

The Little Red Riding Hood is a European folk story that can be traced all the way back to the 10th century. It has many variations, but the core of it is the following. The mother sends her child daughter (teen in some versions with a sexual subtext, but we'll ignore that here) with an errand to her grandma. The way to grandma goes through a dangerous forest and the mother gives her daughter strict instructions to stick to the beaten path, do not stop, do not stray. The daughter, in her childish naivete, fails to do this, gets approached, distracted and fooled by the big bad wolf, who ends up eating both grandmother and granddaughter.

What's the lesson here? Do you need better mothers, able to take better care of their daughters? Do you need better daughters, capable of following sound advice? Do you want to go out and kill all the big bad wolves, so the road can be safe to anyone, regardless of how weak, strong or clueless they are? Do you want to mark the forest as dangerous, ban access into it, and make a road around it?

Replace Little Red Riding hood with the typical employee, the forest with the work environment and the Big Bad Wolf with whatever might happen along the way on the road from idea to intended destination, which is grandma's house. Do you still want to go out and kill all the Big Bad Wolves, make it safe for everyone to wander everywhere without having to fear anything, to overcome anything, to prepare for anything? Remember, we're not talking about kids anymore. Do you want a culture of safety or do you want a culture of strength? Do you want to provide a perfectly tranquil environment where creative whims can flourish, or do you want to provide a competitive environment where weak ideas get filtered out, bad projects fail, and people have to work hard to succeed? The wolf, while scary, has a place in the natural ecosystem and when it is gone, not all that follows is positive. What do you want to do about your wolves and what do you want to teach your Little Red Riding Hoods? Whatever you do, just don't treat them like children. I for one have learned to love the wolf and I've developed an appreciation for a reasonably Darwinian kind of environment, an unsanitized work context where there is still enough unknown and difficulty to create the kind of character and resolve that can move through mountains. Business is not a playground and the occasional sharp corner or sudden step is just fine.

Winners write the history books

Remember the Star Wars example from before? It's instructive from more than one point of view. The latest (as of writing this) Star Wars movie, The Last Jedi, the second of the latest trilogy, is canon. It's a mainline story movie written and launched by the official caretakers of the Star Wars brand and lore, there is no doubt whatsoever on this. And yet, it changed the perspective on some central and beloved characters, compared to previous canon movies, to such a degree that it generated revolt in parts of the fandom. For example, Luke Skywalker was portrayed in a way that many fans felt was unlike Luke, unworthy of Luke, besmirching Luke's memory and ruining his legacy. The actor himself, Mark Hamill, said *"he's not my Luke Skywalker"*. A sort of rebellion ensued, with threats of boycotts and some fans simply declaring that they are refusing to accept this latest trilogy as canon. They will just ignore it and they will consider that the events portrayed here did not happen. Now, I do not have the ambition of being able to solve a Star Wars dispute, that is out of the scope of this book. I am however highlighting that even when you have the formal authority to change the story, if your new story is not received well, you will lose people, as some will stick to the old story, or leave all together.

How do you balance the need to change with the need for stability? Any serious change will leave some people unsatisfied. Trying to not upset anyone is an exercise in paralysis. Real change will break some things, and there will be some people that never want to leave the old story. What do you do? When is it the right time to break with the past, risk losing something old for the promise of gaining something new?

There is no right answer, other than, it's right if it works. If your change leads to success, you will be right. If not, you will be wrong. When Steve Job returned to Apple in 1997, he brutally broke the culture he found there. He quickly moved to fire almost the entire board and put a new one in place. He put new trusted people he brought from NeXT in key positions. He came in with a new vibe and a new plan. He changed the story. Many liked the new story, some didn't and were left behind, fired, or left. As it so happens, he was successful and led Apple to growth unprecedented in the history of capitalism. Had he failed, had he lost too much support back in 1997, had he been left to stand alone, we would now be speaking about the abrasive CEO that did not know how to work with people and drove everyone away, running Apple into the ground. It was right because it worked.

And yes, I know about the outcome bias. This is something else.

Ah, and one more thing. There's one more difference between the Star Wars situation and your company culture. Disney, the current owner of the Star Wars brand doesn't employ the upset fans. The fans are the clients, and that makes a significant difference. Sure, you want your clients part of the brand story as much as anyone else, but the relationship is, while not entirely different, definitely not the same. In the case of your internal culture story, you can't have a group of employees simply deciding to ignore a part of the cultural canon they don't like. Inside the company, cultural adherence is demanded. It also sold, but demanded. Outside the company, there is no demanding, you can only sell.

Trying too hard

Can you try too hard with culture? Yes, you can. Most companies and leaders try too little, but the other way is possible too.

I recently saw a very inspirational commercial, and by inspirational I mean made with that goal in mind, not that it actually inspired, but it had all the trappings: dramatic soundtrack, sunrise, sunflares, a narrator talking about a generation finding its meaning, a country finding its purpose. I think it lasted a whole minute and it kept going on and on about ever bigger things with more and more grandiose statements. No hint of what it was advertising until the very end: Kaufland, a supermarket chain. It fell flat on its face. An overbaked, overdone project taking itself way too seriously, a supermarket trying to solve a generation's and a nation's dilemmas. Do me a favor, have fresher tomatoes on stock and shut up.

I've also seen team leaders trying to take themselves too seriously, coming in one morning and declaring to their team that from now on they will be doing this and that, and only this and that, without having the moral of formal authority to as for any of it. At best they got silence, at worst they got open rebellion. Or maybe silence is worse.

It's a difficult job coming up with cultural stories and demanding adherence. If you don't do any of it, you're abdicating leadership. If you do too much, overstretching your own credibility, you are not taken seriously.

Take the boldest step you can take. If you are a team leader in a company with no strong culture of any kind, starting with something as simple as "disagree and commit" in your team might be transformational. That might be something that matters. Do that, and then figure out and do the next thing. If you're the CEO, you will need to do more, although even then, perhaps even more so, you can easily sound disconnected from reality. Be ambitious, but honest. Own your vulnerabilities. Admit mistakes, but don't give up. Be humble, but unrelenting.

Nothing kills faster than pink elephants

I love the opportunity for willful naivete the consultancy part of my job gives me. I can just go into a company and ask, with apparent well intended childlike wonder: "but why is such and such this way?"; "are you two getting along?"; "are you happy with his performance?"; "what is your greatest fear?".

These simple questions, and others like them, which I almost always am more aware of their importance than I let show, are many times questions that those from inside the company couldn't ask even if they wanted to. It is not really about me, that I am in any way better than them, or more interested in their well being than they themselves are, it is that I have the luxury of being an outsider, of seeing things clearly, and, more importantly, of being free of the constraints they have to contend with, free to ask and say that which they can not anymore, because they've ignored it for too long and it would be too hard to bring it up now, or because of personal histories, or cultural taboos or a million other reasons.

I call these issues pink elephants and whenever I go into a room I look for them first. Lovely animals, it is not their fault, it is the fault of leader, but I'm there to help, because we all have to contend with them once in a while. A pink elephant is an issue, a tension, a problem that, for whatever reason, wasn't addressed in time with Compassionate Radical Honesty, and it has in the meantime become too weird, or painful, or risky, or embarrassing to address. The problem is there, everybody knows it, but nobody names it, they all dance around it. Weird and convoluted conversations take unexpected turns, simple decisions become complicated, people behave in strange ways, all because they are trying to talk about something without talking about it. Like a pink elephant, sitting right there in the room, plainly visible for all, but nobody's saying "hey, we have a pink elephant in the room, right there!". No good leader can tolerate pink elephants in the room. They must be named and addressed right away. It's really hard to do it after you've tolerated them for a long time, but do it you must.

Pink elephants ruin culture faster than most other things, because they are interpreted as weakness, or, worse, hypocrisy and untruthfulness. How can you, the leader, talk about going the extra mile, about rallying around a goal, when there's that pink elephant right there, right in front of you, that you don't dare name? Do not be fooled by the fact that nobody else in the room is not addressing it either, that doesn't mean that they support you. They see it, they see that you see it and they're waiting to take their cues from you. If you do nothing, the only message you're sending is that you're not for real. And if you're not for real, why should they be?

You may not be able to shoo the elephant out of the room, but you still have to address it. The pink elephant in one situation I was involved in was that the head office of a company that had a delivery center here was a mess. A total, undeniable up mess. There was no way to spin it, and, yet, if left unrecognized, it was a culture killing pink elephant. Admitting the problem, admitting that they couldn't fix it from here, not lamenting about it, but accepting it, realistically talking about what they could do, what they did and didn't have control over, and how they could work around it and build something worthwhile despite it, that was what needed to be done. Yes, we can't push this particular elephant out of the room, not for the time being at least, but here he is, and this is what we need to do. That kind of honesty was necessary.

My personality helps me, I like to sense and focus on tensions and surface hidden conflict, get it addressed and resolved. I am not afraid of the fight, I can handle it, I can facilitate it. Maybe your personality doesn't help you with this, but then you need to work more. Not doing it is not an option.

It can be simpler than you think. I once uncovered, in a matter of days, a huge pink elephant that had been sitting there for three years. A simple but clear analysis and recommendation from me, summarized in a couple of pages, unleashed a chain of events that led to the clear and full resolution of the situation. I did not have to push, I did not have to argue. Everybody already knew what I was talking about, they just needed someone to say it plainly.

The criticality of public displays

There's a time for discretion and there's a time for a show. For example, as a leader, you need to always stop mean, abusive behavior right then and there, on the spot, and make a culture building display out of it. Conversely, see heroic behavior and recognize it, on the spot, or at the next all hands or similar opportunity. Which is more important? It's more important to stop abusive behavior. Walking by and doing nothing about it will hurt you more than doing nothing to recognize good work. If you see an asshole manifesting himself by oppressing the weak, this is not the time to be subtle and leave it for a later private conversation. Stop it.

At the same time, please do make sure you don't turn into an oversensitive nanny. Don't jump in to stop any aggression, aggression can be good. Conflict is great. Don't obsesses about leveling the playing field for every little thing. What you need to never tolerate is simple: never allow the powerful to bully, demean and abuse the weak, especially in a way that is personal, that is about a power trip and not the work. At the same time, sure, also teach the weak to stand up for themselves, but that's a different thing and one doesn't excuse the other.

Some decision are just decisions, but some other decisions are precedents. How you decide now, on some apparently simple thing, will be an example and a precedent for your teams. They are watching you, always. I call these decisions culturally loaded decisions. You're in a late evening meeting and you're preparing for an important client visit tomorrow. You went through everything twice already, but you want to check a particular part of the presentation one more time. "Let's leave it, it's good enough, let's go out and have a beer" says a member of your team, a good person otherwise, she had been working hard all day on this. How do you react? Yes, the client visit is likely to be fine anyway and it's unlikely to be made or broken by that slide. But, then again, this is not a merely pragmatic decision, it is a culturally loaded one, small in technical scope as it may be. Do you truly want to obsess about your customers, do you really want this culture? If yes, then you need to insist that the beer will have wait, fur just a bit longer.

It's a great skill for leaders to be quick on their feet because you're going to be faced will all kinds of situations like these where you'll need to respond right then and there in a way that is congruent with your culture and sets the right precedent. Do you have problems doing that, do you freeze, lose your words, don't know what to do? Work on getting better at it and, in the meantime, do what you can. Coming back the next day and saying you know what, we probably should have put in the extra half hour to look at that slide is not as good as having said it then, but it's probably better than never saying it at all. If this is your weakness, not reacting quickly enough, own it, address it, admit it, walk with it, get better and go do the right thing.

Measurements

Few things can be used so right, and so wrong, as business metrics. The brilliant leader will use metrics with the precision and insight of a master swordsman. The bad manager will hide his incompetence and fear in a deluge of numbers. Metrics are the perfect excuse for all mediocrities: we follow the process, we produce the reports, we measure and count things. Measurements: genius in the hands of some, fool's gold in others.

But why? When we build an airplane, we put sensors everywhere and we measure everything. We want to know and control every aspect of its operation. It seems to be such an intuitive thing to do and it seems so weird to say that, as a manager, you shouldn't measure too many things? What gives?

There are two parts to this answer. For one, too much information confuses and ends up reducing performance. Yes, the plane is chock full of sensors, but the design of the cockpit displays and instruments, what exactly to show where, when and how, so the pilots don't get overwhelmed and confused by all this information, is equally as important.

Second, machines and system don't change their behavior when they're measured, but people do.

Netflix, for example, should indeed measure every usage of its streaming services: who watches what, when, for how long, from what device, in what sequence etc. All these things should be measured to death and endlessly tweaked. Netflix, on the other hand, shouldn't apply the same approach to its people, their work and their performance. Code doesn't care if it's measured, it keeps on working just the same. People, on the other hand, are influenced by what and how they are measured on, sometimes drastically so. The key to understanding why measurements can be so useful and also so dangerous, why sometimes they save and sometimes they sink, is to understand that not all measurements are the same and not all situations are the same.

There are three distinct types of metrics:
1. Product metrics. Everything about your product or service being used: who buys it, how, when why, how does it get used, how does it work, when it breaks down.
2. People metrics. How you define individual performance and how you measure it.
3. Organizational metrics. How your teams, departments and business units organize, focus their energies, spend resources and work to deliver business results.

The first kind of metrics, product metrics, should be done to your maximum practical ability to do it, there's no real downside to having as much as possible, if you have the bandwidth to process them. Learn everything you can about who and why and how buys and uses your product or service, fill it with sensors, live diagnostic tools, collect usage data, do everything you can to gain insights that will give you that extra edge: how are you competing, what you need to fix first, what you need to build next, who's your customer and what do they want.

The second kind of metric, people metrics, is itself of three different types.

When it comes to complex research problems, like coming up with a novel technical solution or a new kind of product, we have people engaged in difficult and exploratory work, solving non-trivial problems, outputting results in a nonlinear way. They could be trying ideas and prototypes for months, producing nothing usable in the meantime, discarding idea after idea, and then apparently out of nowhere come up with the right design that will be the basis for a killer product. Some other times, nothing useful at all is going to come out of it. How do you measure the performance of one of the members of such a team? Do you measure the hours they put in? Do you measure the number of experiments they perform per day or week? Any such measurement will risk being a blunt instrument and do more harm than good by confusing, demotivating and even angering your valuable employees. What you need here is a clear story of performance, a set of principle and leaders you can trust, with measurements coming in at a distant second. For the sake of clarity, I am in no way saying that this kind of work is so precious that it needs to be insulated from business realities. No. You may want to instill a great sense of urgency in such a team. You may come with a hard deadline and push them to do their best within the time they have. You may do all kinds of things, but whatever you do, you need to understand that simple, repetitive, productivity type of measurements are not going to be the answer in this particular case.

A second, rather different scenario, is executives and senior managers. Life is not simpler for these people, maybe from the contrary, but unlike the researchers from the previous example, these people are hired, and paid, to deliver on numbers no matter what, because the buck has to stop somewhere. The head of sales needs to sell. The head of engineering needs to build things. Executives and senior managers need to have clear numbers and they need to be held accountable to them. These numbers should be very few, very clear, and, usually, outcome oriented. Don't measure the process, the activity, measure the result. They will in turn measure the process and the activity in their areas because it helps them understand how to optimize their internal organizations, but you, as their leader, you need to ask for results. Results and culture, that's what you want: results delivered while enhancing the culture you want.

The third and most common category is what I call predictable knowledge work, for example a team of software developers from an outsourcing company building a mobile banking app for one of their clients. It is highly qualified, hard work and the project can and will hit many unexpected problems, but, research it is not. It's been done before, there are precedents and best practices to follow. It's a complicated problem, but it's not a complex problem. The work is predictable enough that you can, given conditions of stability, expect linear output, sprint by sprint, or month by month, at team level. The work is however not predictable enough to measure it daily and at an individual level. Attempting to measure, for example, the output of every individual member of the team, every day, in terms of features delivered, is unwise. You may have the most experienced member of the team investing a large part of her day helping more junior members and also electing to work on the most complicated features, which take the most time and have the highest degree of uncertainty. Measuring this person on features delivered day in day out, without understanding the other kinds of value she is delivering, is myopic, demotivating and counterproductive.

When it comes to people, you want executives and senior managers that can deliver on numbers, but you want them to do it without simply and blindly cascading more and more numbers below until they suffocate the organization. You also need to distinguish between complex and complicated problems and understand that measurements will need to adjust accordingly. I'm using complex and complicated in the Cynefin sense of the word.

Continuing with the third and final kind of business metric, the organizational measurements, we go back to an area where you'd like to know as much as possible, but it's very important what you do with what you find out. Profit, revenue, margins, profit per business line/product, revenue per employee, customer lifetime value, customer acquisition cost, average tenure of employee, attrition, cost of replacement, recruiting lead time, and many others, all these are organizational metrics. These are the kind of metrics that can tell you if the company as a whole is doing ok, how are you competing, what divisions/products are profitable, what's working and what not. These metrics give you insights that could lead to entering or exiting markets, changing products, or reorganizing internally, introducing new practices and discontinuing existing ones. The danger here is misunderstanding, paralysis, reacting to the wrong things in the wrong way. However, that aside, you do want as much of these as practically possible, but be prepared to separate the noise from the signal and make decisions without getting stuck in the weeds.

To summarize:
- Product metrics: the more the merrier, understand everything, leave no stone unturned.
- People metrics: they can wreck your culture, have few, be careful, rely more on leadership and a performance story rather than people productivity metrics. See Performance in Step 6 for more.
- Organizational metrics: have them, use them, don't get lost in them, know how to stop analyzing and make decisions.

How exactly do measurements wreck culture and kill teams?

One of the most widely disparaged human resources policies was Microsoft's stack ranking, discontinued in 2013. Under stack ranking, each manager had to put her employees on a scale and she had to declare a certain fixed percentage of each in a performance category. In other words, there had for example to be a bottom category of underperformers that were punished, even if she genuinely felt that everybody in her team did a good job. Conversely, there was only so much space at the top, even if more than a few team members performed outstandingly. This drove a counter-productive competitive atmosphere where good performers were not incentivized to invest time to help struggling team mates and where excellent performers avoided working in the same team with other excellent performers, as they didn't want competition for the top positions. All kinds of perverse behaviors came about as an unintended result of implementing stack ranking. Nobody wanted this to happen, but it did happen, and it poisoned the company culture for years. Microsoft wasn't alone in implement this kind of policy, fashionable for a while after having been popularized in the 80's by Jack Welch at General Electric under his famous 20/70/10: lavish your top 20% performers with rewards, give very little to your mid 70% and tell them to get into the 20% if they want more, and fire your bottom 10%. What may have worked for Jack and his factories in the 80's is not working in the knowledge industry of the 21st century.

Process heavy annual performance measurements are another kind of, mostly negative, measurements. The forced artificiality of SMART objectives, the fake game of gathering feedback once a year for events long passed and faded from memory, it all leads to a wasteful and sour dance from which neither managers nor employees come out winning. I will detail how to do this right in the Performance chapter, under Step 6.

The problem with measurements and the reason why they can easily wreck your culture is that when you mess with people's livelihood, with their compensation, with their motivation, status, and professional pride by measuring their work and performance, they react, and they react instantly and forcefully. If you get it just right, they will react as you intended them to. If you don't, they will react in all the ways you didn't want them to react and you didn't even think it was possible for them to react like that, but they will. It is very difficult to get it right and the more measurements you have, the harder it is. This is definitely a place where you want to keep it simple and focus on leadership, on example, on a culture of transparency, accountability and constant feedback, rather than on measurements.

Example from my experience.

You promise a team a bonus if they finish ahead of time. Intended outcome: they finish faster. Unintended but real outcome: shortcuts are taken, quality drops.

You promise a team a bonus if they finish ahead of time, this time before they start the project. Intended outcome: they finish faster. Unintended but real outcome: they will give you ridiculously high estimates and they will refuse to take any risk, in effect guaranteeing that they will finish ahead of time, i.e. ahead of their own estimates.

You promise a team a bonus if they have fewer than x bugs of a certain severity or higher. Intended outcome: the product has fewer bugs. Unintended but real outcome: the team ferociously argues every bug instead of just fixing it and moving on. It's not a bug, it's a feature. It wasn't clear in the requirement. It is of a lower severity.

Yes, good people, in a healthy culture, may resist these impulses and may not give in to these counterproductive behaviors. For a while, yes, but persist with your unwise measurements, and you won't have a healthy culture anymore, your good people will leave or adapt to the new diminished reality and you will find yourself policing your own teams, a sad state of affairs indeed.

The other important question is, what are you measuring for?

There are three reason why you might want to measure anything:
- Measure to know
- Measure to nudge
- Measure to enforce

Measure to know. This is the big data approach, the Google approach. You want to have as many data points about everything whatsoever and slice and dice them in all possible ways. There is no direct and immediate relationship between measurement and action: you may act on it, most of the times you won't, not right away or not at all. You just want to know and see later what you do with all this knowledge. Done in this way, you can obsessively measure everything, including the individual performance of your people and, as long as you don't do it intrusively, you don't bother them with it and you don't overreact, you won't wreck your culture. It's expensive to do, getting cheaper though, it risks creating a culture of over-analysis, but it can be done.

Measure to nudge. Taking a cue from behavioral economics and particularly from Nobel prize winner Richard Thaler's work, co-author of the "Nudge: Improving Decisions About Health, Wealth, and Happiness" book, this is what he called the paternalistic libertarian approach: you would like to guide people towards the decisions you think are best for them, but you don't want to enforce or restrict, you only want to nudge. You've measured that many of your developers don't do unit testing and you'd like more of them to do it, so you go ahead and nudge them in that direction: you market the advantages of it, you highlight examples of it being successfully used, you praise those that do it. You sell your idea internally in your company to your developers, you make it easy, you make it attractive, but you don't enforce. You can usually safely nudge without wrecking your culture.

Measure to enforce. The traditional management philosophy. Taking the unit testing example, you go ahead and set a rule: everybody needs to do it. Come performance evaluation time, you will measure if they did it and, if they didn't, they will get a bad grade in some category or another. Or, even more directly, you implement a code review policy and no code is accepted unless it comes with unit testing. These are the kind of measurements that can easily wreck your culture if you don't do it right. Be careful with them.

Of course, you could do it all. Measure everything just to know, have the big data approach. Out of that big pile of insights, extract some things that you deem relevant and urgent enough and off the back of that nudge certain people towards certain behaviors. On some, even fewer, absolutely critical items, go as far as enforcing. If you don't have the resources to do it all, then my simple rule of thumb is this: enforce product measurements, enforce key organizational measurements, enforce executive and senior manager measurements, and nudge people behaviors through measurements. In all situations, enforced or nudged, don't try to do too many things at the same time. Pick and prioritize. Conflicting rules will cancel each other out and generate distraction, frustration and inefficiency. People can effectively focus on only so many things at the same time. Confuse them with too many targets and objectives and KPI's and you will get worse and worse performance.

Minimal rules

One of the best examples you can use to come up with a set of rules or guidelines to run your business is the common law, which is the Anglo-Saxon legal system as it emerged and developed since the middle ages. It is an uncodified system. Texts exist, of course, more so in modern time, but there is no requirement nor ambition that there is "one big book" of all the laws, unified under one big symmetric overarching architecture. Common law starts with simple statements that sound more like principles, without any detailed implementation instructions attached. For example, let's take the principle of private property as it might have emerged in its first, very simple and primitive form: the owner of a piece of land can do as he wishes with it. For a while, this principle is enough, and people farm and use their land, and everyone understands what private property means and there is peace and harmony. Sometime later, let's say that a particular land owner, John, gets the bright idea to build a dam and stop a river running through his land, so he can collect more water and better irrigate his fields. Neighboring landowners protest: the river is not John's alone they say, the river springs from outside his lands, from way up in the hills, and it flows through all the fields, watering the entire valley. The river, they argue, while passing through their individual parcels of land, is at the same time a kind of common property and one person can not use it all for his needs. John disagrees. He does not care where the river comes from, or what it does before it reaches his lands, but once on his lands, he is free to build dams and do whatever else he likes, he argues.

We now have a conflict. The initial statement of what private property means, while sufficient for a time, is not enough anymore, because we now have a situation that is ambiguous and undefined and there are two or more people with opposite opinions butting heads. Fortunately, there is a conflict resolution system as well, in the case of common law being the courts, with judge and jury. The parties will take their conflict before a court of law and the court will decide one way or another, for example it will decide against John and determine that a landowner can not simply dam and stop a river. This decision, once made in a court of law, becomes precedent and it has legal value. All other similar disputes in other places, between other parties, will now look at this precedent and follow it. Precedents can be adjusted by a subsequent court decision, they can even be overturned, but they are not lightly overturned.

Conflict in this way is not a problem but expected and it is the key learning and continuous improvement mechanism. We just need to make sure we keep it civil and in the courts, not violent and in the streets.

The key thing with common law is that it's emerging, it's the kind of legislation that is just in time, just enough. Potential ambiguity exists all the time in its statements, but this ambiguity is solved only when it becomes real, that is when two opposing parties bring a conflict before a court of law, and then a decision is made, and a precedent established. Ambiguity is not solved proactively, there's nobody legislating before there is a need to legislate, because the simplicity and readability of the laws is deemed important and they are not complicated unnecessarily.

You want a clean fridge in the office. Simple statement: keep the fridge clean please, or we will. Every Friday, you throw out food left there by the employees, so it doesn't get spoiled over the weekend. It works well, until one particular Monday, one particular employee comes complaining that his food was thrown out and he didn't know that would happen and he had some good stuff in there. Now we have conflict. The simple statement of keeping the fridge clean is not enough anymore. What is your conflict resolution process? Let's say it's your decision, as the office manager. What precedent do you want to establish? What is the simplest, smallest, most minimal, least invasive thing you can do? You put a sticker on the fridge: "every Friday, 7 PM, we will empty the fridge and throw away anything we find inside". Ambiguity removed, problem solved, for a while, until it will need further improvement.

I was once working with my team on a learning process, trying to figure out how to let people pick and choose courses and what not. At first, we tried to come up with rigorous process and document it in detail: who should say what to whom, when, what information should be given exactly, what would be the flow of approval, the steps. It all got really complicated really fast, and we realized we were the ones overcomplicating it, so we wised up and went the common law way. Instead of a complex set of intricate rules, we simply said "express your interest to the learning coordinator". We didn't say how, we didn't say when, we didn't give them a template to fill. This would be enough for now. If and when it will fail, either through conflict or through volume, we will take another look and maybe improve it. Until them, and maybe forever, "please express your interest" would be just fine.

When you create processes and rules and guidelines, do not attempt to solve and prevent all the problems you can imagine potentially happening. Legislate minimally, have the simplest and least restrictive set of rules you can have. Establish a clear conflict resolution process (even if it's as simple as escalation to you), make it clear, and let it go. Conflict will happen, but conflict is proof of what you really need to fix, not what you would have imagined you need to fix. Faced with conflict, decide, set a precedent, a minimally intrusive precedent, and move on, until the next conflict, and the next precedent, and so on, and so on.

Why you can't have your cake and eat it too

A tendency some managers have is that they try to do both things. Both sides of every coin, both approaches to every dilemma. Do you want a culture of quick risky decisions or one of exhaustive deliberation? Well, you say, I want both, depending on the situation. No shit you want both, depending on the situation. Who doesn't. Problem is, with culture, you have to pick, and if you don't pick, you risk losing it all.

Unlike pragmatic, number driven management decisions, culture is a mixture of storytelling, lore, marketing, PR, routines, precedents and taboos, and these things work differently than numbers. When you calculate a budget you can say that exactly 43.7% will go to this and 25.9% will go to that. When it comes to culture, when it comes to making people care about it, hear it, pay attention, understand it, adhere to it, live it, you need to inspire and you need clear, attractive messages, and a message of we'll do a bit of everything depending on what the situation asks for is none of the above and that's why it's a terrible culture message. Culture tends to deal in absolutes, so people can see what you stand for and see that you're standing for something, whatever that is, that you're showing courage, because courage is always an endearing leadership quality.

I always said that I want a loud culture, a culture where people speak up and everyone, at every level, takes the initiative, owns their career and grabs their manager and asks for what they need. Did I not also then speak with the managers and asked them to also do the opposite thing, to pay attention to their people, to ask and to probe? Of course I did, because some people are too shy to be loud, and I knew that, they would need a helping hand. But, when it came to culture, when it came to the big public statement, I couldn't go there and see "you do a bit of speaking up please, and we'll do a bit of listening, and we may end up somewhere in the middle". I couldn't do that because that wasn't going to inspire anyone, and also because that's not what I wanted. I truly and genuinely wanted a loud culture, with people taking ownership of their situation, and I wanted to move them towards that, get them out of their comfort zone. I recognized that the situation will never be ideal and that it would get a while to make real progress, but culturally speaking, there was not much room for nuances.

The big cultural statements are almost never nuanced. The stories and lore that get built around them, including the fanfiction, almost always are. A nice exception to this is the agile manifesto: *"Individuals and interactions over processes and tools"* they say in one of four such statements, and they explain it like this: *"That is, while there is value in the items on the right, we value the items on the left more."* It works, and it worked for the agile movement especially, which, at the time, had the great challenge of changing established mindsets and creeping into the enterprise. It was the smart thing for them to recognize the value in existing systems, while at the same time saying that there's a better way, because they needed to sell into existing systems.

I like nuances, I am a big fan of sophistication, but when it comes to culture, I will urge you to err towards simplicity. Culture is not that place where you're trying to make everyone happy and cover all real life use cases. Culture is that place where you're pointing to a bright and shiny destination and you're saying "this is who we are, and that's where we're going".

Stand for something obvious and burn all bridges

When I was the manager at Endava Iași, I decided, with my team, that we would not do counter offers. If someone valuable wanted to leave, and they had a better financial offer from another company, and they were professional and civil about it, we would try to keep them, discuss their career, potentially have them do new things, understand their point of view, work together on a plan. We would discuss money too, yes, but only in terms of the likelihood of future promotions and raises if things went well, no promises, and definitely no counter offers on the spot.

Once we made this decision, we had a choice. Do we communicate this policy, or do we keep it secret, a practice of ours, the management team, that we follow discreetly? What should we do? The careful, cautious manager would probably choose to keep it secret, because that would give him flexibility. If you keep it secret, then you do your best to abide by it, as much as you can, but if sometimes the situation demands an exception, you can make it without any reputation loss, because nobody even knows you made an exception. That would be the cautious thing to do, some would say even reasonable, prudent. We did the exact opposite. I spoke publicly about this rule of ours, again and again. We didn't write it in any official policy because official policies weren't for that, but I made it clear that was what we were going to behave like. I made myself vulnerable on purpose. If I was to ever make a counter offer, word would spread, and I would be seen as a liar and weak leader, and that's exactly what I wanted. Not that I didn't trust myself to stay true to a private decision, but when it comes to leadership, sometimes it's better to burn your bridges, and burn them publicly, so everyone can see what you're willing to do.

Later on, years later, we softened the rule and we made a few exceptions, and accordingly communicated the change in mindset, but by then we had the discipline throughout the larger team and we had proven our point.

Not everything you do needs to be a public promise, a bridge burned, a display of will. Do it for the things that matter, the pain points, the culture defining questions. Back then, as it is now also, companies were frequently weak and caved in to threats of resignation, and that encouraged a culture that we didn't like or want. Employees were aware of that and it was even a practice for some, not all by all means, to get raises: they threatened to leave. In their defense, there were managers, or at least the widespread perception that there were managers, in some companies, that did not give significant raises to those quietly working hard and waiting to be observed, but only to those that forced them, by threatening to quit. It was important for us to not encourage that kind of behavior in our people, and, also, to differentiate ourselves from other companies by showing willingness to publicly stand by such a policy. We didn't do this for every decision we made or for every management practice we had. Most of our decisions were not secret, we would answer if asked, we would inform the relevant groups, but they weren't important enough to make a big deal out of them by widely and proactively communicating them to all.

Politics and bad apples

Politics in business has two definitions. One, that could be seen as positive, is the ability to gather support for your initiatives, through your communication, relationships and PR skills.

The other, which is horrible, is getting a career advantage or benefit through means other than delivering and behaving according to the priorities of the business.

The second kind of politics, the bad kind, is really bad and is culture killing. Because the word itself is confusing, I don't like to use it in the "good" sense, so I call the ability to gather support for your initiatives in the right way influence, and, in a business context, politics always has a bad connotation for me. There is no right kind of politics and, as a leader, you should actively work to wipe it out.

Apart from not actually engaging in it or encouraging it, you need to do the following:
- Firmly and swiftly discourage it in others, doubly so in your direct reports.
- Go the extra mile to make sure that certain actions of yours are not seen as political, even if your intention was not political; perception is reality and if you are seen as a political animal, you are a political animal.

The moment someone comes to you to complain about a co-worker, what do you do? You want to listen, because they might be bringing up a real problem, and you want to be a good guy, the good boss, but can you listen too carefully and be too sympathetic, more than you should? If Mike comes to complain about Anne's behavior, and you spend an hour talking to him, in private, what message do you send? Is Mike going to assume you agree with him, even if you didn't explicitly say so, because, after all, you spent all this time listening to him complain? Is Anne, seeing you through the glass walls of the conference room, going to assume he's gotten a hold of your ear first and she lost? You are, inadvertently, being political, by sending the wrong message, and are encouraging political behavior. The right way to do it is to spend 5 minutes with Mike: Is this an ongoing situation right now that demands immediate and forceful intervention? If not, have you already told her this feedback as well? Why not? I will arrange a meeting with you two that I will moderate, and you will have to raise your points to her.

Rooting out politics requires more than simply not engaging in it, it requires deliberate transparency and behaviors that make it explicit it's not going to be tolerated, and it's not going to work.

I once had a conflict between a hard headed strong delivery person that overworked his people into the ground and a weak, lying leader, that was loved by his team, because he never pushed them. I fired the liar because by lying and being weak he was being political and ruining the culture. I told the maniac he had to take it slower or else, but that I understood that what he did he did out in the open, transparently, for the greater good, and that earned him a kind of respect and a second chance. I told each of them why I did what I did, and I told my team why I did what I did, because the why was important.

People should never have to worry about who's having lunch with you. Access to you shouldn't be a shortcut or a detour from the one thing you'd like everyone to know: influence comes through performance, not proximity to the boss. Control your biases, inform yourself from more than one source, don't overreact, keep your cool.

Bad apples are almost always political apples. Some also deliver, some don't. Bad apples ruin a team, ruin a culture, ruin your sanity. Bad apples don't want to get better. They will find a reason not to change and the fault will always be with someone else. Bad apples don't value feedback and bad apples don't know how to put the team ahead of their own needs. There is no good reason to keep a bad apple.

Culture tools

Example is the most important culture tool. Your people look at you, their people look at them. Nothing is more important, and example always trumps words.

Decisions are important, and so is your decision architecture. What are you nudging people towards through the systems and processes you've put in place?

Your public communication is also important. Newsletters, all hands, celebrations. Use the opportunity to broadcast key messages.

You can also deep dive. Go personally to look at a detail, levels below you. Spend half a day in a particular corner of your business. Learn something and create a story that will be told long after you leave that corner.

Last but not least, your reputation, which will, indeed, precede you. Use it if it helps, make sure to change it if you need to, but know it's there.

Step 6: Building fluent teams

Fluent teams

Look everywhere you see great success and you will find a great team. Even the most mercurial leaders, the most outsized personalities, the most difficult CEO's will more often than not have a great team around them.

What is a team? In one sense of the word, a team is a small group of people working together on the same thing and, under this loose definition, the world is full of teams, but that's not the definition I follow. A bunch of people put together and given a project to deliver are not, just like that, a team, they're just people assigned to the same task, with the same boss.

A team, in my definition, is a group of people that care about the same thing more than they care about their individual needs. A team always has a leader and a fluent team, which is my understanding of a great team, is a team whose members talk honestly and make decisions effectively.

There are many ways to look at a team, many ways in which teams work, succeed and fail, and apparently contradictory lessons can be extracted from the examples of legendary teams, but also from our own teams, or the team across the hallway. Sports and the military are also great places to study teams, because teams are so explicit there, organized in very obvious ways, with standard sizes and structures, following stricter rules of engagement than in business. I've read my fair share of military lessons, but I prefer to focus on business examples, as they are the actual thing I'm writing about.

Bad Teams

Here's an example of a bad team. You have the business unit manager, or the site manager, and to her report all the functional managers, or, if it's a mission organization, the heads of accounts or projects. You've got her and her team of say the head of engineering, the head of project management, the HR head, the finance head and so on and they're her team and she's the leader. At the beginning of the year she gets some objectives from headquarters and she breaks them down by area to each member of her team. If the objective is growth, then HR will have to hire x people, engineering will have to be able to spin up y teams and so on. They all push back and negotiate as much as they can, to minimize the scope of what they have to do. Once the objectives are settled, they start delivering. The need to collaborate is small so they don't. It's not that it would be bad if they did, but because they are so siloed, they've evolved into a working mode where they don't and when they do it's, at best, a side thing to their main work or, at worst, a turf war. When they get together for the weekly operational meeting, they are there as representatives of their respective constituencies, pushing their departments' agendas, juggling for favors and influence with the boss. When it comes to promotions and raises, they're all working to get a bigger slice of the pie, at the expense of the others, with no real incentive or inclination to really consider the good of the whole above the good of their turfs. This is not a good team, this is a bad team, this is a bunch of managers coming together at the behest of a bigger manager, fighting each other for influence and resources. A group of people, even bound together by the same overall objectives and reporting to the same boss, don't necessarily a team make. Whenever this happens, it is, first and foremost, a failure of leadership. Yes, the structure may incentivize unhealthy behaviors as well but it is a leadership responsibility to create a real team out of a group of people that just happen to share a plan and some resources.

Another example of an often bad team is the Scrum team. In theory, in Scrum you have The Team, which is pretty much everyone, and it's organized as an egalitarian, consensus based group, where nobody has any formal authority over anyone else. You then have the Scrum Master, one person who's the servant leader, the remover of impediments, someone making sure the process is followed and The Team has all it needs to do its job and it's working efficiently, but the Scrum Master can't tell The Team as a whole or any member The Team to do or not do anything, they can only suggest. The last one is the Product Owner, who represents the client and who comes up with the requirements, prioritized and explained for The Team, so they know what they need to do. He can't impose deadlines on the team, he can only impose the order in which stuff gets done. The Scrum Master has a clear role, the Product Owner has the clearest role of them all, but The Team is left to self organize and that's nice and noble, but what I see in many of these teams, again and again, is vacuum of accountability and vacuum of leadership, leading to tolerance of bad performance, lowered standards and frustration. Let's assume we have 5 developers in The Team, one very senior hard working person, very nice guy, almost shy, two medium experienced hard working people, a lazy slacker and a distracted junior in need of guidance. The slacker is going to avoid work, will not do his fair share and will, to put it bluntly, bullshit his way through meetings, avoiding accountability. Who's going to take care of the problem? The senior developer won't do it, he has no experience at all in dealing with these kinds of issues, he's soft, he doesn't know what do to with it, so he lets the pink elephant be. The two hard working developers don't like the slacker's attitude, they make a few jokes, poke him a bit, but he shakes it off, so they give up, they're not there to educate him, they just want to get their work done and get to go home at a reasonable hour. The junior looks around, see this dysfunctional team, understanding or not what's happening, he still gets to be influenced by it, tries to learn something, maybe he gets to, maybe he doesn't. What's supposed to happen, who's supposed to fix this team? The Scrum Master you say? Ok, let's assume that we have a component and observant Scrum Master, and she sees the problem and tries to fix it. Thing is, as the Scrum Master, she has no authority to do anything. She can talk to the slacker, she can ask him to change, she can try to persuade him, but she can't actually demand anything. What if he just ignores her, what then? Who's going to take care of the situation? This is where we get to the dirty little secret of Scrum, which is that what happens right now in most places when problems like these happen is that it's escalated to some kind of manager outside of Scrum, a people manager of some sort, who has the power to demand and to punish, if she needs to. Scrum's insistence on a lack of clear and unambiguous leadership in the team only works because, when the team is lucky to have good, well intended members, it works, not at its full potential, but well enough to not attract attention, and Scrum gets the credit. When it doesn't work, when you hit the hard people issues, Scrum can't fix its own mess and it falls back to the "real" management behind it, the people that can actually do something about an issue. I find this situation somewhat hypocritical and I think that methodologies like Scrum have a lot of good ideas baked into them, but the naïve insistence on completely self organizing teams is not one of them.

I don't think leaderless teams work. I have never seen or heard of a leaderless team that did anything above, at best, being competent. Any team that I have seen or read about that ever did something worthwhile had a leader. Yes, we prefer modern leaders, empowering, flexible, and we prefer mature team members that do not need to be led in detail, sure, but a leader there always needs to be. Even in Scrum teams where, in theory, there is no leader, a leader emerges, be it an informal one, but nonetheless serving the same purpose and doing the same job. With precious few exceptions, so few as to not be of practical importance, hierarchies emerge even when they are not formally imposed or even when they are formally discouraged. I find no virtue in denying this reality of human nature for the sake of the ideological purpose of a leaderless team. Yes, nobody wants Dilbert style managers cluelessly imposed from above and, in principle, management should be reduced to its absolute minimum, but teams do need leaders. Do you want to let them emerge, have them rise to the top, just for the sake of avoiding any shred of formal leadership? Fine, do that, but understand the penalty you'll pay in inefficient decision making and slow progress and the high likelihood of failed and mediocre teams.

Any team needs three things

Any fluent team needs three things. It needs safety, so people can be themselves, take risks and have the mental and emotional space to proactively do stuff. A team also needs Compassion Radical Honesty, so it can always speak the truth and improve itself. Radical Honesty is not only a relationship tool, or a decisions tool, it's also a continuous improvement tool, through which the team sees new information, discusses it, integrates it and demands performance from each other. And, finally, a team also needs a journey, which is the big picture, the vision, and every journey is made up of two parts: a destination and a way of getting there.

Behind safety there is trust, because where there is no trust, there is no safety and there is no honesty. People can trust each other in two different ways: they can have predictive trust, that is, be able to anticipate their teammates' behaviors in hypothetical situations, and they can also have safety trust, trust that their teammates will have their back no matter what. Safety trust grows off the back of predictive trust, but it's not a one to one relationship and one doesn't guarantee the other.

Safety

Safety should not be confused with niceness, a culture of gratuitous support or lax standards. Aggressive, conflictual and dynamic teams can also be very safe. I feel safer, in the team sense of the word, in the sense of being at ease and myself, with my aggressive business partners that I know and trust, than I feel with some very soft spoken and polite people that I don't know enough to implicitly trust. Aggressiveness and trust are two different things, and safety is more of a function of trust than niceness.

A team is safe for each and every one of its members when, no matter how bad she fucks up, she will always be able to count on her team to be honest and transparent with her. The one thing she will not have to ever fear is being talked about behind her back by her teammates. Second, the team is focused on fixing the situation and helping her. I am not saying that the team will not be upset but, fundamentally, the focus is constructive. Last but not least, if the team decides to forgive and still wants her in the team, which will be situation for most mistakes aside from the most grievous ones, then the team will truly forgive, there is no lingering bad blood.

Just to be clear, safety is not the absence of consequence, including and up to firing someone if no other option is possible. It's also not easy forgiveness, or the absence of rebuke or negative feedback, nor is it the absence of hard work and difficult challenges. Team safety is the presence of honesty and the sincere intention of everyone to act in the best interest of the team, with no personal grudges, ego in check, to forgive as much as possible, to teach as much as possible, to encourage as much as possible. What "as much as possible" means differs from team to team.

In this way, no matter how demanding a safe team might be, no matter how bumpy the road, the experience of being part of one is always remembered as a time of honesty, of people trying to do their best, interested in building something together, not in politics, not in ego trips or other petty interests.

In a team I led, I established it to be safe to contradict anyone on anything, including me, the leader, in as a direct and blunt way as anyone wanted. Of course, the bluntness went both ways: everyone gave as good as they got, but, at the end of the day, nobody worried what their teammates thought about them. Each of us knew where we stood, and we trusted each other that whatever we had to say, we could said it.

In another team I led I established it that it was safe to try and fail, even by making decisions solo, without checking with me, as long as reasonable preparation was made. I would not punish honest attempts at something that failed, but I would not tolerate people rolling the dice, trying something out on a whim without even a modicum of thought. Specifically, I was trying to teach my people, people managers themselves, to not be afraid to establish clear expectations with their people, even if that meant that some people would leave. In this talent starved market, managers tend to be artificially nice and be afraid to push their people towards real performance for fear of them simply leaving to any of the many other companies that would hire them on the spot. I told them to make a real, honest attempt at understanding everyone, their needs, aspirations, gripes and wants. I told them to care for every one of their people but, at the same time, establish clear, non negotiable expectations of what was wanted of them. If someone would have a problem with that, explain it to them, make sure they understood what and why we were asking them to do, but fundamentally, some things were not negotiable and if someone felt they couldn't work like that and had to leave, then let them leave. No bad blood, but no passionate attempt to keep them either. Some people did indeed leave and I backed my words with action: I kept calm, I kept it cool, I never blamed my team and when we discussed situations we discussed to learn from them, not to find fault.

All I wanted from my people was an honest attempt at doing their best and as long as they did that, I had nothing to complain about. It was up to me to point them into the right direction.

I did not have anyone in my team that intentionally broke the expectations contract, that for example went into a meeting with an employee and was on purpose mean and petty. If I had, that would not have been trying their best. That would have been an outright and frontal challenge to the values of the team, and a direct insult to myself as the leader and, more importantly, to the team. Intentions matter. People genuinely trying to do the right thing can be forgiven a million times and taught to do better. People trying to intentionally piss the couch in order to get attention, and in the process showing contempt for the values of the team and for the wellbeing of their teammates, these people should be rarely, if ever, forgiven. I've had situations where I had to remove people that had all the right intentions but just couldn't, repeatedly, deliver, but they were far fewer than situations where people had the skills, but the wrong intentions.

Fewer things piss me off more than leaders that do not give their teams the respect, courtesy and trust of being in their corner and not speaking badly about them behind their backs. When a team has such a coward of a leader, how can you expect anything but an unhealthy work environment and, ultimately, failure?

So, if your boss asks you about your team, what do you do? Do you lie and tell him that everything is great and everyone is doing great? Do you hide all problems? No, you don't have to do that. You can, in confidence, share a summary of your assessment of your team members. You can also share your concerns about some of them, such that you may have. You however only share the real concerns, and you do it professionally, with respect, giving them the benefit of a doubt, making sure to not paint an overly dark picture of them in the eyes of your boss, crippling their career chances in the process. You can talk about the strengths and weaknesses of your team and its members to your boss, or even your peers, in confidence, that is not gossiping, that is actually good management, but you do it respectfully and evenly. What you never do is complain about them in any kind of gossipy, exaggerated, mean, tabloid style, because that is wrong, and it hurts them, and it makes you look weak and mean, and you never criticize them in random situations, to random people, just because you felt like complaining about something. You don't complain about your team, you make it better, you change it, you accept it, or you quit, but you don't complain like you're on the outside looking in, you're the leader of that team! How can you complain about something that you are responsible for like it was someone else's problems? That is not leadership.

CRH in the team

Compassionate Radical Honesty is also a team tool, not only a one to one tool. CRH is how the leader, and every member of the team, raises issues, discusses, gives feedback, pushes ahead. The daily team meeting, the weekly operational meeting, the project meetings, the informal interactions, they're all CRH infused.

As the leader you use CRH in a team setting to get clear information and straight answers. You use it to push and challenge where you're not getting what you need. You use it to assign accountability, to ask for deadlines and to challenge your people to perform.

The old adage of "praise in public, criticize in private" is mostly true: sensitive personal feedback should be given in private. However, instant feedback on someone's work and contribution can and should be given in public, even if it is not praise, in a CRH way: "you said it was going to be done today, what happened?"; "you can do better than this, this is unfinished". Radically honest teams will have this kind of conversations with ease, in front of each other. The intention of these questions will not be to make someone feel bad, or to blow some steam off, but to demand performance, to raise the standard and to hold each other accountable.

It is a leader's job to always be on the lookout for conversational complacency, which is what happens when a tired, disengaged, bored or simply too polite team avoids the real issues and skims across the surface of the problem space for fear of upsetting each other. When you see that, your job is to insist, to push, to go deep in search of the critical questions and the real debates. If you sense the group is avoiding tension, more often than not, your job is to surface that tension and put it on the table, feelings be damned. There are many reasons to postpone and avoid a difficult group conversation, and they are all easy to understand and very human indeed, but you must resist them. Instinctively, most of us want to keep the peace, to keep the harmony. Compassionate Radical Honesty is the unnatural act of not doing that and it's an endurance game, you need to do it and keep doing it, until it becomes second nature. You have to keep at it every day, because once you relax it, it's instantly visible, and the team relaxes, and standards go down.

To achieve CRH on a particular issue can take from a second and a glance to hours and days of ferocious debate. When I had to tell someone in my team I expected more from them the what they just delivered, I did it. If they challenged my position, and I welcomed the challenge, we would continue to debate it then and there, lively and energetically, until the issue was thoroughly discussed, with the rest of the team usually chiming in. I would not shy away from describing what their work lacked, and if we had to leave that meeting feeling a bit raw, that was the price we both paid, knowing it was for the best and that, in the end, it would strengthen our relationship. These debates could go on for hours, derailing the whole meeting and then some. As important as it was to not waste our energies arguing trivialities, it was equally important to debate the real issues until a deep decision could be made.

On the other hand, there were also times when Compassionate Radical Honesty could be achieved in a couple of seconds and with just a few words. I remember an incident in a project when a very junior member made a stupid technical mistake, something really embarrassing, but something that could happen to anyone. We were all gathered for the team meeting and we instantly realized his mistake, and it was instantly obvious too, by how he turned red and struggled to find his next words, that he had also fully realized what he had done. No further CRH action was required. He was already regretting it in all possible ways and the learning opportunity was already realized. The rest of us were also aware of the situation and spending more time on it then and there would have served little purpose but to unnecessarily embarrass him. Honesty, personal and at a team level, was achieved without the need to push for it. We simply agreed who was going to help him fix it and moved on to the next item on the agenda.

Getting personal

What do you do when you sense that someone in your team has problems outside of work that he carries over to work? What do you do when someone in your team seems to be going through a tough time and might be able to use the kind of help that can't simply be expressed in business terms, by talking about the work. How personal do you get? Here is how I look at it.

First, don't overestimate your skill at reading people. We all are programmed to jump to conclusions so make sure you don't do that. You may think you've understood what's going on, but don't be too confident that you did, treat your intuition as a hypothesis.

Second, don't barge into anyone's personal space. Don't jump straight into a radically personal topic out of the blue. Even if you guessed it right and even if they need the help you think they need, they probably don't want it in an invasive way. I've had a few people I came across that looked deep into my eyes, thought they saw something they recognized and then started playing armchair psychologist with me, thinking they might blow my mind. I remember most of them as insufferable fools.

What I always appreciate, and what I always offer, is a respectful helping hand. At the right time, in a private context, I will ask a question like "It seems to me that you have been on the edge these past few weeks, sensitive to criticism, ready to jump, volatile. I don't want to get into anything that is too personal or that doesn't concern me, but I want to ask if I can help". I explicitly ask for permission to get involved and make it very easy for them to say no. I then shut up and let them talk and they now have the choice to get as personal as they want to and even if they don't do it now, they still know that door is going to be open in the future, if they want it. I've expressed the issue in mostly business terms, but I've opened up the idea that, if it needs to be discussed in broader terms than that, I'm willing. Alternatively, if you're not willing, say it. Tell them that you see this problem at work, tell them you don't want to get into their personal life, and that you are willing to do what you can do professionally to help them, but the problem needs to get fixed.

What do you do if they don't take your offer to discuss in more personal terms, but the work problem still doesn't get fixed? You have to insist on the work problem getting fixed. Show them compassion but give them radical honesty: you need them to understand what's not working and you need them to fix it. Do they need some days where they won't be able to give it 100%, because of reasons they don't want to say? Sure, give it to them, you don't need to know. Trust them, if you see them trying. All in all, now or later, but not too late, the work problem needs to get fixed. It's up to them if they also want to ask your advice on the corresponding personal problem, if you're open to that, that is.

What do you do when they get more personal than you want them to? I once had a guy who, after telling me a long and very personal story of how he broke up with his ex-wife and how it was her fault, asked me to pay part of his salary off the books, so he wouldn't have to pay as high of an alimony. That was definitely more personal than I wanted or needed. I've had other people that acted very familiar to me and wanted to hang out, go out for beers, spend time together. I didn't take it against them and it didn't upset or offend me in any way, but at the same time I wasn't looking for new friends and I'm not in the habit of having random beers, so I had to say no.

Sometimes, one of your people may develop a crush on you and put out romantic signals. Whatever it may be, you decide what your boundary is, communicate it and stick to it. Mine is somewhat beyond the professional, you can ask me for a personal favor, if I can I'll do it, if you want some advice I'll give it, but I don't have time for the messiness that comes with people that really don't know how to set and keep to their own boundaries. I also have a small number of very close professional partners where the boundaries are very different indeed, but that's a different kind of relationship.

Who's taking the puppy home?

Compassionate Radical Honesty in a team is great because it surfaces tension, clarifies and strengthens relationships and drives pink elephants away. Its ultimate desired manifestation however is in effective decision making and in results. Real decision making and results require determination, commitment and accountability.

In my early days, I tended to do a lot, be everywhere. I was there with my teams, debating, discussing, engaging, on the frontlines. It was therefore very frustrating to see how often good people didn't deliver on their word, people whose good intentions I fully trusted. Something was missing. We were putting in the effort, we were putting in the heart, but the traction wasn't there. We were routinely failing to get things done at the rate which I would have expected, given how hard we worked.

It was, of course, my fault. I was failing at CRH by not clearly stating what I wanted, by not making people give precise commitments and by not confronting them directly when they didn't deliver. I did it out of a bias: myself, I valued independence and freedom above anything else, and I compulsively had to give it to everyone around me, without realizing that we're not all the same and, even those of my team mates who valued their autonomy as highly as I did, they might still have needed more specific guidance, simply because they were in a different stage of their career, on a different point on the learning curve. I preferred loose ambitious objectives with no detail, but other people wanted clearer assignments with specific deadlines. Telling people what to do in such a directive way felt like a failure of imagination, like a bad shortcut, like a more primitive kind of leadership and, for the longest time, I could not do it. It is still not my preferred tool, but I now know how and when to use it, and I do. I may very well have also had that most common fear leaders have: the fear that people won't actually follow them. That's why some leaders don't challenge, that's why they don't ask for more, that's why they don't confront, because they are afraid that by doing that they will shatter the illusion that their people are actually willing to go the extra mile for them. A pleasant lie is, often and sadly, preferred over a risky reality check.

It was even more frustrating as I did a lot of the right things: I addressed the core issues, I engaged in the long exhausting debates, only to then slip and mess it up in the final minutes, sabotaging my own hard work. When it came to closing, when it came to establishing clear and precise accountability, I failed. I blinked, I muddled the message, I let it ambiguous, I asked them to try, they said they would, none of us knew what that meant, it wasn't serious, it was confusing and meaningless, and that's why I wasn't getting traction, because I wasn't closing my conversations by appointing or otherwise arriving to clear and specific individual accountability.

My breakthrough came at the end of one long day when I suddenly pictured every issue that came up in the discussion as a puppy, a shelter puppy right there on the table, in the middle of us, looking up with his puppy eyes, wanting nothing more than to be taken home by one of us, adopted, loved and taken care of.

Who was going to take the puppy home? That was the question. Who was going to take accountability for caring for that puppy right there, no matter what? Discussion that did not end in clear accountability was chatter about the puppy without actually doing anything for him. We were just wasting our time talking about dogs we were going to do nothing about. Worse still, it made us feel good. Simply debating, engaging, released enough stress to make us feel like we had done something, but we hadn't. A day of talking about puppies felt like actually taking one home, and that was wrong, because it was an illusion and no puppy had been rescued.

Ever since that day, I always ask: who's taking the puppy home? Otherwise, let's just call this a brainstorming conversation and not pretend we're making any decisions here, because we aren't. Along the same lines, I tend to react poorly to passive voice, plurals and third person: something should be done, we should do that, that would be good. Who exactly is "we" and what does it mean that it "should" be done, how exactly does that work? Give me a name, tell me what you'll do by when, and now you're talking.

The Journey

There's something about movement that is difficult to put in numbers, but it makes all the difference. Stagnation is depressing, you need to be going somewhere, working towards something, and there is so much more than the pursuing the actual objective, it's opportunity, it's excitement, it's development.

Warriors in peace time get rusty and get bored. Good developers wasted on maintenance work get demotivated. Companies that peddle around still water, with no clear purpose or direction, don't tend to attract a lot of excitement. When stuff happens, there are new things to do, people move around, they try something new, junior members of the team get to step up, everyone is better off.

The team needs to be on a journey and a full journey has a destination and a way of getting there.

The destination is likely to be incomplete, changing and evolving. It is by now common knowledge that the contemporary business world moves fast, and that companies and teams need to be agile, forever adapting to changing realities, constantly adjusting their plans and strategies. Books such as "The Lean Startup" address this in brilliant detail. At a project level, methodologies such as Scrum solve the same problem and when it comes to this, the iterative approach, they do it well. When I therefore say that you need to give your team a destination, we both understand that you are unlikely to be able to give them a precisely detailed destination. Surprisingly, this is less of a problem than it might seem. More importantly than a precise destination, you owe them an inspiring destination, a bold statement of some sort that means something. By talking about the destination, I'm not trying to solve a planning need. You will solve your planning need some other way. I am trying to solve a purpose need. The team needs a purpose. Why are they doing what they are doing, and what are they doing? Your job, as a leader, is to give your team a destination in the sense that it gives them the emotional drive to understand why they're coming to work, other than for a paycheck.

A good destination has three components to it:
1. It is ambitious, but realistic.
2. It is specific enough to mean something, but aspirational enough to be more than a list of features of some system or product you're building.
3. It is easy to understand, clearly communicated, and often repeated, until it is understood and embedded in everyone's decision making.

I used to work with teams developing bits of huge financial systems, in collaboration with teams from the client and other suppliers. A destination that meant something wasn't an easy thing to find. We weren't making a physical thing that you could touch. We weren't building a specific website that was going to solve a specific need, with a clear brand. Instead, we might have been working on a core banking system of some sort to adapt it to some changes in the Russian legislation or what not and to produce some new types of reports, alongside the hundreds of types of existing reports. The system was going to be used not by the general public, but by a small number of internal users, which we rarely got to speak to directly. Regardless, hard as it was, a destination we had to have so we did all we could to get one. We tried to understand as much as we could about the intended benefit of the changes, the key reason behind the required feature set. We got as much input as we could from people as close as possible to the real users. We identified what was hard about what we were doing, what was going to be the key to success. We put all these together in a destination story that, while not the most exciting thing ever, made sense, and it mattered.

When I say that, alongside a destination, a team needs a way to get there, I am, again, not simply referring to a plan, but more to a set of behaviors that answer the question: "on the way to this destination of ours, how are we going to work together and how are we going to treat each other, as we overcome obstacles and challenges?" A way of getting there is made up of:
- A decision making process.
- Clear accountabilities.
- Safety.
- And yes, a plan, not in the technical sense necessarily, but enough to make people believe that the destination is reachable and to give them a direction.

"We're going to put quality above anything else" is a destination, not a project destination, but an organizational destination. This is a real, mostly failed example, that I saw with my own eyes, the story of a company wide initiative on quality that was loudly announced, from the highest levels, in not many more words than that: we want quality. The typical questions that pop into peoples' heads when you say something like that are along the lines of "What does it mean? Why do we want to do it, what's the problem with how we do it now? Will we introduce some new quality processes in the development practices? Do we know which? Are they going to be enforced? How? Is anyone in charge of this? When do we start? When do we expect to finish? When it gets to delicate decisions, such as taking the time for quality vs delivering fast to an eager client, how do we choose?". As a leader, if you communicate an initiative like this to your company, be ready to follow-up right away with some kind of answers to these questions, even before the questions are asked. The answers don't have to be all detailed and finely calculated, but the main ideas need to be there. People need to understand what it means, give them a taste, a feeling for it. In our case, there wasn't much except the first general statement so, on first hearing, it didn't seem real, it seemed more like a vague intention that might turn into something real, at some point in the future, maybe, but we'll worry about it when we get there. We'll worry about it when it gets real is the death sentence of any company or team initiative. The worry about it when we get there is a fine philosophy for technical decisions, but team and cultural changes need to be done with a sense of urgency, they must be immediate, unavoidable, too big to ignore, or they will be ignored.

"I want us, in this team, to get to a point where each of us is autonomous and enabled to make decisions in their area quickly, boldly and effectively". This is an example of a team destination. Through a statement like this you, as the leader, are effectively kicking off a team transformation. How are we going to get there? Some of us will surely be stretched. We are going to support each other and I, as the leader, will personally coach each and every one of you through this. What happens if we make mistakes along the way? We will have to learn new ways to organize ourselves and to behave, and we'll do that together. Where do we start? We'll have a kick off meeting on Monday where I'll go through all of this in some more detail, some general directions I have in mind, and I want you to come prepared with questions. How is this unavoidable? We will have a 6 months timebox by which this change needs to be done and we'll draft our plan with that in mind, and we'll track our progress on a weekly basis, with bigger monthly milestones. These are the kinds of questions and answers you will need to address as part of this journey.

As the leader, it is your responsibility to ensure that your team has a full journey, and that means two things: a destination, but also a way of getting there.

Decisions: Consensus vs leader, slow vs fast, facts vs guts

The decision making process of a fluent team should be explicitly discussed and agreed. It may emerge organically, it may change in time, but it should be clear and explicit to the team. In many ways, it matters less how exactly you make decisions than making sure everyone knows how it's done. Every single member of the team should know what needs to happen in order for a decision to be made, they should understand when a decision was made, and they should know how to get to a decision when they want one made.

Some teams may say that all decisions need to be approved by the leader. It's a simple enough process. Bring your proposal to the leader and if she says yes, go do it, if not, not.

Some teams will want to delegate responsibility by function or area or up to a certain level of expenditure or scope, below which decisions can be made without checking with the leader.

Some teams will agree to discuss all major decisions at their Monday team meeting and, if some new significant decision needs to be made during the week, they'll have a quick huddle.

Many different decision making processes are possible. Some are faster, some are more comprehensive, some are centralized, some are consensus or majority based, some are formal and written, some are informal and conversational. Different environment will benefit from different decision making processes. An internet startup will want a fast, risk tolerant decision making process. A pharma company will want a safe, risk averse decision making process.

For all and any situation, three things stay true:
1. Every team member should have a clear understanding of how decisions are made and what's expected of her.
2. Every team member should have an opportunity to voice her opinion; a degree of decision making efficiency may have to be sacrificed for the sake of deep buy in. How much and in what way, it varies.
3. When a decision is made, all team members equally and fully support it, no matter if, during the deliberation phase, they agreed with it or not. This is the disagree and commit principle.

Another important aspect to consider is if decisions should be postponed as much as possible, or, from the contrary, made as soon as they can be made. The lean school of thought, the agile approach, is to postpone. Just in time, just enough, is doing things not a moment sooner than you have to and doing the minimum necessary. The idea is to avoid over engineering, of doing too much before you know for sure what's needed, and therefore wasting effort, time, money and opportunity. You want to avoid waste at all costs, so you postpone until you're sure and even then, you do the least you can do. There is definitely value in this approach, especially when it comes to what I call routine investment decisions. Should you build feature A or feature B? Should you market to public A or public B? Before going all in, do test it, try it, prototype it, do all the lean stuff, break the big decision down in many smaller decisions, fragment risk and postpone the point of no return to as far in the future as possible. On other hand, as a leader, you also have what I call culture decisions: how do you hire, how do you reward, what behaviors do you want to see, what behaviors do you stop, how do you interact, how do you discuss, how is feedback given etc. When it comes to culture decisions, a different logic applies as it's not anymore about minimizing waste and making sure you're not investing effort too early, but about communicating clear messages and about setting the right examples for your team. When it comes to culture decisions, make them as early as you can, as forcefully as you need to, and do not postpone. It makes sense to wait and ponder features, it doesn't make sense to wait and ponder values, as values should be clear from the start. The other problem with a pure lean/agile approach of decision postponement is that it's an approach well suited for incremental improvement and sustaining innovation, but not for radical innovation, but as this is a leadership book and not an innovation book, I won't go into detail on that here. I will simply say that radical innovation is usually not about minimizing risk, but about maximizing opportunity for discovery.

When it comes to facts vs guts, how should you lean? You have a decision to make, how much do you dig for numbers and how much do you ask for opinions? First, understand the nature of the decision at hand, figure out how quantifiable it is. If you're talking about a test strategy for example, then it's very worthwhile to get as many facts as you can: what kind of bugs have we had in the past, in what area, any patterns we can observe, what are the trends, how much did we spend to fix them, etc. This is an example of a decision you can make in a reasonably scientific way, by aiming to inform yourself with objective data and then letting the data speak for itself. This is not the same as analysis paralysis and I'm not saying you need perfect data, that's not the key point I'm making here, the key point I'm making is that all those involved in this discussion accept the fundamentally objective nature of the decision they have to make and are doing their best to think scientifically, driven by the facts. This is not a decision where opinions, feelings or values have much of role to play, it's a technical decision. Let's take another example and say that you are deciding if you want to push hard for a culture of ownership and accountability. Discussion and debate in the team is still necessary and valuable, but it's a different kind of debate. In this situation, there will be bits and pieces of objective data, studies, some personal anecdotes, but you can't really hope to decide in a definitive way if your idea is the one right idea. Compared to what? It's still worthwhile to discuss all the objective information you have, to imagine scenarios, to challenge each other, but, unlike the test strategy decision, fundamentally you can't hope to scientifically reach the one true answer here, as there probably isn't such an answer at all, or if there is, it's completely beyond your ability to measure and calculate. Those involved in this discussion understand that, at the end of the day, this is the kind of decision that will be informed by facts but made on values and personal preference, and that's fine, as long as you understand this, and you own it. To summarize, when you can get to the one true answer, go for it, but when you can't, accept it and make the decision on something else, own it and run with it. It's very useful for any team to understand and decide among themselves what kind of the decision are they trying to reach, facts or guts, so there's no confusion.

It is, as always, the responsibility of the leader to make sure all this is in place.

Suffocating authority vs liberating authority

A lot of what's happening now, and has been happening for some decades, on the frontlines of management thinking and organizational design is a fight against overbearing hierarchy and against debilitating bureaucracy and, from my point of view, it's been a great thing. However, I think a confusion is being made: the opposite of the traditional, rigidly hierarchical management is not necessarily an egalitarian culture.

The core of the problem is what I call suffocating authority, which is the kind of authority that drains your emotional well-being and stifles your initiatives. Bureaucracy that makes all initiatives dull and complicated beyond reasonable effort. Make your people jump through unnecessary hoops to get anything done, and they won't get anything done. People understand doing what needs to be done for the work to be good, but they smell bureaucratic bullshit a mile away. Byzantine decision making processes where you have be a politician simply to get your routine work done are the death sentence for any company that wants to compete in today's world. Worse of all, a kind of authority of the leader where personal deference is expected, that is guaranteed stagnation. Even with ferocious leaders like Steve Jobs, who was a force of nature and you didn't want to get on his bad side, if you really knew what you were saying, you could stand your ground and contradict him, and he would end up agreeing with you. It wasn't a gentle process but, in the end, ideas won. Ideas above leaders, no matter how good those leaders may be.

Leaders that have big egos and are vindictive create suffocating authority. Leaders that belittle and bully are suffocating their teams. Leaders that don't speak their mind, that play and encourage politics, that don't work to establish clear and transparent decision making processes, that don't give honest feedback, they are all suffocating. Suffocating authority is poison. I once had a leader in a team, indirectly reporting to me and he was, for lack of a better word, a coward. He did not have the guts to tell his people what he thought about them, but he complained about them all the time behind their backs. He did not have the guts to establish a clear operating model for the team, so nobody ever knew what decision was being made, and how. Weak leaders can be suffocatingly authoritative too, it's not just the powerful callous types. In my experience, bad leadership comes out of weakness just as often or more as it comes from excessive ego or authority. I worry about the decisions of weak people more than I worry about the decisions of strong people.

Liberating authority on the other hand is the kind of authority that makes people feel good and lets them do things. Authority is great.

Authority is the ability and confidence to make decisions and see them through. Our challenge is not to restrict authority, but to make it honest, fair and effective, and to delegate it as close to the action as possible: decisions should be made, whenever possible, by those who get to directly live with them. Coders should make decisions about code. Testers about tests. Designers about design. Etc.

Your challenge as a leader is not to diminish your own authority, or the authority of others and to create some kind of hippie consensus culture where nobody can do anything without the gently obtained consent of everyone else and their mothers. From the contrary, you need to continuously work to increase your authority and the authority of everyone in your team, but of the liberating kind. You need to be able to make bigger and bolder decisions every day, easier, faster every time, and you want people in your team that grow in the same way.

Make it transparent, be compassionately and radically honest, establish a clear decision making process, do it for the good of the team, be ethical. Suffocating authority is a zero sum game: the more I have, the less for you. Liberating authority is the opposite: the more I have, the more I can help you get some too.

Be a strong leader and use your strength to make something great happen.

Dishonest relationships

I once had in a team of mine two senior people, each in charge of an important functional area. They both had strong personalities and had a history of butting heads, but, largely, it had been constructive, and they had shown, on more than one occasion, that they could work together. Until they couldn't, that is. I started noticing more and more that conversations between them, on fairly routine topics that came up in our weekly team operational meeting, were getting ridiculously complicated. Topics that I would expect to get decided in a matter of minutes dragged on for hours, derailing the whole meeting. When I tried to figure it out, to understand the problem, I had this weird slippery feeling, like every question I asked created more confusion and I didn't understand why. I didn't understand what was so difficult or tricky about the things they were arguing about. It all seemed rather simple to me and it should have been easy for them too, but, obviously, it wasn't.

The problem was that their professional relationship had become dishonest. They had issues, resentments, they had pink elephants they couldn't speak about, they had things to say to each that they didn't, and all that tension was surfacing as a bad attitude that was compromising their ability to get anything done. Those issues they were arguing about that seemed simple to me, they really were simple. The reason they couldn't get past them was that they their resentment towards each other was surfacing in unrelated conversations, making everything else more difficult than it had to be. Were they doing it on purpose, or was it simply an emotional tension that clouded their vision? A mix of both probably.

I first tried to solve the problem logically. Ok I said, maybe your responsibilities are overlapping and it's not clear who should do what, so let's clarify them. Let's restate the purpose of what we're trying to do. It didn't work, because that was not the issue. I had to realize the problem was deeper and engage with each of them, in 1-1s, in some compassionate radical honesty, telling them how it felt from my side, how it wasn't ok, that I was sensing some deeper tension, and asking them to tell me what was really going on. It wasn't easy, they had some tricky things to work through, but once the relationships was fixed and it became honest again, the specific issues got exponentially easier to address, communication improved drastically, decision making got way better, and the team got a lot more fluent.

A habit of mental poverty

I was working with a leadership team once that was going through a bad time. Good people were leaving the company, hiring was hard and, as the top team was too busy struggling with its own internal problems and dysfunctions, it was having a tough time addressing the issues. I won't get into why they were where they were, it doesn't matter. The key point is that, for months, they had been struggling with each other and the situation in their company. When I started working with them, I sometimes felt like we were planning a funeral. They had some real assets as a company and they had some great people, but everything felt like a problem and everyone spent time arguing why everything was difficult. I call it a culture of mental poverty because it felt like what they were doing what scrounging for dimes and nickels and they couldn't get enough to afford anything of what they needed, only that they weren't talking about money, but about their confidence in themselves, in each other and in the people around them. That was their currency.

The worst thing was that these weren't bad people, they were good people, but the team was bad and they had forgotten how to win, as a team.

If you find yourself arguing against your own self interest, trying to convince others or yourself why you can't win anything, why the competition has all the advantages, why you're stuck, then you've fallen victim to a culture of mental poverty. The way to get out of it is to take a step back and start doing things, anything, move, act. Stop trying to plan to ensure success, that's a loser's game, there's never such a thing such as ensuring anything. Action is the antidote to mental poverty.

The neat car syndrome

There's this guy I see almost every day, couple of streets from me, constantly cleaning and working on his white BMW. It's a spotless car. Not one speck of dust, not one forgotten coffee cup inside, nothing there that shouldn't be there. The car looks great, like it just rolled out of the showroom.

I only hope he gets to use that car half as much as he gets to clean it. Mine on the other hand, is a mess. The outside is scratched, and the inside is used and abused. The back seats are full of dog hair, from Brodie. The volume wheel is missing, so I control it from the steering wheel. Every nook and cranny is dusty. The windows haven't been perfectly transparent for years. The engine however works perfectly, I've always taken care of it. The brake pads are new and so are the tires. More importantly, I've been to the Atlantic Ocean and back with it, tent in the trunk, on the road day in, day out. My car is for driving and whatever dings or scratches or dirt it has to get as part of taking me places, so be it.

Leaders can sometimes treat their teams like a car they're obsessed with keeping neat, putting all their focus and energy into organizing the team, its ceremonies, its processes, its routines, making everything run perfectly smooth, with no extra motion and no delay. Sure, some degree of organization is required, but they should be careful not to end up like my white BMW guy, putting more time in polishing that thing than in using it to go places. A car is meant to take you somewhere and a team is meant to do things. Stop polishing and do something. Your job as a leader is not to have the neatest team, this is not a beauty contest. Your job as a leader is to take your team to interesting places.

Drive & motivation

Let's define drive as that combination of factors which makes people do things voluntarily, above what's directly asked of them and beyond what structure and process force them to do.

I see drive as a triangle of motivation, determination and time. Motivation is the desire to do something, the good feeling you have about an activity, the fact that you like doing it, it pumps you up, puts a smile on your face just thinking about it, you're eager to get started and you look forward to the result. Determination is the grit and persistence to keep going, to do the less pleasant parts of your job, and do them competently, to persevere through the tough times, to be professional even on those days when you don't feel like even getting out of bed. Time is the great secret and it's really all about control, and time is the most important kind of control.

Control is the difference between working 12-hour days on something that you love and that you chose, and feeling physically exhausted but mentally recharged and happy, and working 8-hour days on things that are imposed on you, that you don't understand why you're doing, that you can't predict or influence, and then feeling sapped and sad. When you lack control, everything feels bad, even if it's objectively good, if it's decent work, decently paid. When you have control, you're ready to face any challenge, no matter how difficult. What is control? There is no objective definition of control, and, in a way, I'd better call it the feeling of control, as that would be more accurate. Few of us really control all of what we do, as things come up, are asked of us and situations change, but we need enough control, we need the feeling of control. The easiest and most important place to start is to get control is your time. Plan your week. Plan your day. Focus on your important tasks. Negotiate what's asked of you. Each Sunday, or Monday morning, I plan the key activities for my week. I don't plan every hour, I just list 5 or so key results I want to get that week. Taken together, they usually take between 10 and 30 hours, so they're between 25% and 50% of my week. The rest is for the things I have to do, such as already agreed work, already set meetings, and for the unforeseen. Then, every morning, before anything else, I plan the day. I take what I can from those weekly key results and plan some of them for that day. I revisit, confirm, refresh my meetings and other activities. Even during the course of a day things change, but when they do, I negotiate the change. If someone asks something of me, I don't just say yes, I clarify to understand what's needed, maybe it can be done later, maybe it doesn't need a meeting, maybe an email will do, maybe I don't want and need to do it at all. As I work on things, I don't let myself be interrupted. My phone is always on mute and I never answer it when I'm focused on something and I also try to avoid looking at my email and messages until I finish the current task and I'm in between periods of focus, periods which usually take between 30 and 60 minutes, though sometimes significantly longer. As I read emails and messages, I am careful to not compulsively react to them immediately and derail my day. In this way, I am flexible and ready for change, but I am also in control, as much as I need and want to do be, because any change, small or large, I control in the sense that I understand, I negotiate, and I fit into my priorities in a deliberate way. Controlling your time is a great place to start taking control of your work, of your life. You're unlikely to ever control all of your time, or even most of it, but start with something. Start with 10 minutes in the morning that are yours and yours alone, where you, by yourself, plan your day, and don't let anyone take that away from you. Start with that.

When it comes to pure motivation, to that feeling of enjoying your work, today's accepted wisdom is Dan Pink's triad, which I like but also want to add to it, and to an extent challenge it. Pink's key assertion is that, once we get over the hygiene factors, such as physical safety and a decent wage, more money doesn't help, and what motivates us additionally from that point onwards is mastery, autonomy and purpose. A 2010 Princeton University study, analyzing responses from 450.000 Americans, put that number at 75.000 dollar a year, for the average American. Others however, looking at the problem in a different way, came up with 100 million in net worth in order to live the fullest possible life as a New Yorker. Warren Buffett said he would be happy with 100k a year. Maybe he would, he's famously modest.

I've been a big fan of Pink's theory and, on one level, there's no contradicting it, it's only natural to give people room to be themselves, let them get good at their craft, tell them what going on, so they know what's happening. It's not easy to do this, it's a hard thing, as a manager, pressed by deadlines, budgets and all the other things, to actually understand and do the daily actions that give your people the space, the tools and the freedom they need to practice their mastery, their autonomy, and have a purpose. It's not enough to simply understand it, even want it, you have to make it happen, day in, day out, through well done delegation, through good communication, through feedback. Being wise is only half the story. Applied wisdom is the other.

What Pink's approach misses is determination, the utility of negative motivation and the true power of cash. Ah, and it misses the magical power of obsession.

I think about determination in its stoic meaning: keep walking, no matter what, keep walking. You overcome obstacles, you endure, you keep pushing, you keep moving. The concept of grit, as explained these days by Angela Duckworth, is a good approximation of this and it focuses on perseverance, a sense of duty, on just getting it done.

We therefore constantly work with two types of, contradictory, motivational drivers. On one hand, you need to believe that, largely speaking, you're working towards something that's worth your time and effort, as life is too short to waste. This is the "what's in it for me" voice, this is you looking to know it's going to be worth it. On the other hand, and somehow opposed with the "what's in it for me" voice, as a day to day attitude, you need determination. You have an overall purpose, but you won't find pure pleasure and meaning in every little thing you do every day. Some of the work is going to be boring, some of it is going to be hard, some of it is going to be lonely. You need to keep moving, through pain, towards your purpose. The hedonistic illusion that everything should always feel great and new and fresh is just that, an illusion, and a dangerous one at that. This is your determination voice and you need to balance it with your what's in it for me voice. On a big scale, years, your "what's in it for me" voice should win. You should invest your time in causes you can believe in and in teams where you're going to be properly appreciated and rewarded. On a small scale, your determination voice should win. You will have good days, you will have bad days, but you need to keep moving. The local optimum feeling of each day, each hour, is not the same as the larger optimum for a full year. The best year is not a series of the best days. The best year may include some sacrifice and some pain in some large parts of that year, but it may be a great year nonetheless, more than other more conventionally pleasant years, because you may have learned something important, or achieved something worthwhile. Don't take crap every day, again and again, in the hope of a bright future that might never come. But the exact opposite, packing your toys and leaving at the first sign of trouble, is equally silly. Don't refuse to invest in a future, to sacrifice for a plan, simply because you want to, like a child, feel good every single moment, doing every single thing. If you know what you're working for and why, stick to it for a while.

Determination is achieved through self discipline, through a firm but constructive attitude, through focus, through honesty, through good relationships with your colleagues, through respect for your clients, by simply doing a good job, no matter what you do. Stop waiting to wake up one day and magically feel great, out of nowhere. Make your bed, brew your coffee, brush your teeth and go do your thing and do it well right now, today, feelings be damned.

Negative emotion is also a valid motivation technique, if used ethically, not to attack, not as a power game, not to gain an upper hand on someone or to crush someone's hopes. Negative emotion with positive intent behind it, because we need to understand what happens if we fail. Yes, we don't need to obsess about it, we don't need to get so scared by the thought of failure until we can't act anymore, but we need to understand what happens if we fail, not only what happens if we succeed. If the ring is delivered to Mordor and destroyed, Sauron is defeated, and we shall have peace in the world. If we fail to destroy the ring, we are all dead and the world turns to shit. You can't have one without the other, you can't just talk about the upside, about the positive scenario and its rewards, you need to also talk about what happens if we don't make it and full motivation is only possible with both. We are driven by what we can gain, but we are also driven by what we could lose. Rarely does the fate of the world hang on the outcome of our work, but even so, there are things we can lose. I was once involved, temporarily, as a team lead, in a project developing a piece of a financial system for a huge bank. It was our first piece of work for them and our big chance to gain credibility and potentially get a lot more work from them. It was strategically important for the company as a whole that we do well because our growth plans relied, at that moment, on this bank. You can bet I made sure the team understood what we had to lose if we failed. Yes, I kept an overall positive tone, I encouraged, supported, led by example, because it was a really difficult project and a very difficult client, it wasn't like every other day I would go back to "scaring" my team with the negative scenario. No, and scaring anyone wasn't the point, but a serious conversation in the start, and a few times more during critical points, about what we stood to win and to lose, that we had.

On a more personal level, people can sometimes be so blind to what they're doing wrong, so sure of themselves, so ready to argue feedback away, that a positive way to spin it, a constructive way to give feedback as they say it, just doesn't get through. In these cases, you need to deliberately create negative emotion in these people, shock them, because that's the only way you'll be able to get to them. Make them vividly understand what they stand to lose, the promotion they could miss, the raise they might not get, the reputation damage they might suffer, the job they might eventually lose, if they don't get their act together, and when you have to do something like this, don't try to make a shit sandwich out of it. Shit sandwich is what Ben Horowitz calls the sandwich feedback technique: something nice (bread), the shit in the middle, something nice again (the other bread). This is no time for childish games, this is the time to get straight to them with a clear, direct and poignant message. You can talk about the positive, the upside, the next day, after they went home and thought really hard about what you told them, because you have someone you can talk to now.

But probably the most important motivational factor is who you are, as a leader, and how your team is organized and how it works. Good leadership, honest and moral leadership, competent leadership, a team with a clear journey, with a code of conduct, a well running team that knows where it's going, that's going to be a great motivator for anyone.

The true power of cash. There's nothing like money: it is the clearest, most quantifiable, most fungible kind of reward. Yes, a culture focused too much money and money used as a lazy substitute for the other kind of stuff we all need, such as meaning, professional pride and all the other things, that's not what you want. You don't want money to shortcut the other important conversations but jumping to the other extreme and saying that money doesn't matter, that's it's a kind of "dirty" motivation, that's just plain silly. If you don't know the power of a hefty bonus or a serious raise, you probably haven't given, or received, too many of them. There's nothing like cash. If you have it, don't abuse it, and don't use it to get out of the difficult conversations you need to have as a leader anyway, but don't be afraid to think and talk money. Money matters, and it matters beyond the hygiene factor.

The magic of obsession. Obsession is so powerful that it should be banned. It's like a performance enhancing drug, it's so strong it's not fair, but there are two kinds of obsession, and only one is helpful. There's the ruminating obsession, when you obsess about the past, what you did or didn't do and worry out of your wits about things you can't control. This is destructive obsession and it won't make you better. And then there's future oriented obsession, where you love something so much, where you are compelled to do something to such a degree that you are fueled with all the motivation, grit and passion you could ever want. You are not balanced in your obsession, obsession is not 9 to 5 and it doesn't take long lunch breaks. I am writing this exact sentence at 4:09 AM on a Sunday night, 36 hours after having run a mountain half marathon, and at 8 AM I will be leaving to do a full day workshop with a startup. 6 hours ago, I had a choice: do I play a bit of Witcher before going to bed, or do I write? I did not need to write and there was nothing standing in the way of me enjoying myself a bit and not doing any work at all tonight. I had no immediate deadline, I had no impending delivery, and yet I chose to write and I'm still writing, 6 hours later, knowing I will have a tough time waking up, but I have to do it, because once I start it I can't stop until I'm spent. This is the story of my life: a series of long days, excesses, taking myself too far, learning, getting better in the process. What makes me do this, what makes me wake up on a Saturday morning and practically write non stop until Monday, with a crashing kind of sleep in between and maybe a run at some weird hour, to clear my mind? I do it because I am obsessed by my work, because I need to get it done, because I love every minute of it, and there's no way I will stop to smell the roses or to have a beer with friends or whatever the so called balance implies. And what I also know about myself is that it will never be done. Once I finish this book, there will be something else and I will have to obsess about that too, because that's just who I am. What I've also learned, in time, was how to stop my obsession from turning into perfectionism and how to, when needed, make it client friendly. How to obsess with a deadline and with good communication, because raw obsession, seen from the outside, is scary and unpredictable. I obsess professionally in my commercial work, but I also have my personal projects, like writing this book here, where I go all out and there's nothing balanced, it's all sweet bliss.

How do you, as a leader, energize a team that needs energizing?

First and foremost, you use CRH to recognize and spell out all the hygiene issues, and all the other issues. Fix as many of them as you can quickly, but before too long, move to the next stage, even if you haven't fixed everything. Give it a quick once over. Fix only what you must before moving ahead, there is no perfect moment when everything is great and then and only then real work begins, that's a dream, an illusion, so don't wait for it to come. Fixing problems is a journey, not a destination, and work happens as you fix problems, not after. The horizon is not real, there is no end to the rainbow where everything is solved. The determination and motivation of your team needs to start happening now, not at some hypothetical time when everything around it will be great. Show grit through personal example. Be there, show that you care, be determined, take chances, care about your people, put in the work. Lead by example. Next, talk about motivation. Don't hold a big speech, take it one step at a time. Tell them, what are you doing there? Provide clarity. Organize things a little bit. That's great motivation. Talk about the goal of the project, of whatever you're doing. Stretch your people a bit, find the right work for them. Address all of Pink's triad: mastery, autonomy, and purpose. Help them get control of their time, teach them to plan their work, teach them to say no, to negotiate. Be authentic and vulnerable as you do it, admit what you have, what you don't, start from something and build on it. Talk about what you stand to lose. Use negative emotion if you have to. Pay them well, to the best of your abilities and according to what they should be paid, and fight for their raises and bonuses.

Another topic I would like to quickly address is manipulation, which is a silly red herring. Manipulation is to managers what sex is to sixth graders: they like to talk about it because they think it makes them cool, but they don't understand it. Yes, you can manipulate people, and by that I mean playing to their emotions and expectations to make them do something, while avoiding the difficult issue you would have had to otherwise address head on. I can manipulate, you can manipulate, he can manipulate, she can manipulate, it's no big deal. There's no mystery about it, do it, see how it feels, get over it and then start being a real leader.

Performance

United States Supreme Court Justice Potter Stewart once referred to hard core pornography, by saying that he can't come up with a scientific definition of what it is and isn't, but *"I'll know it when I see it"*. Performance can be surprisingly similar.

Yes, at the executive level, numbers will tell a lot of the story. The company needs to make a profit and profit can be easily measured. The company needs to sell, and sales can be easily measured. This kind of outcome performance, where we look at the output and see if it is where it should be is the way in which we measure the performance of organizations in the grand scale of things. I call it the stock market mentality: we look at some numbers, we look at trends and we decide if we invest. Understanding what's under the hood is, from a level of abstraction above, optional. It is a valid high level view of performance because, in the end, success will be reflected in the numbers, but it's not a complete understanding of performance, because it has no predictive value.

Outcome performance can and is frequently also applied to smaller units and on more intermediary measurements. Is the division making its fair share of profit to contribute to the overall company results? Is the team delivering on time? Does the project have a sufficiently small number of bugs? The problem with this kind of smaller and smaller outcome measurements is twofold. For one, the numbers at this level are more and more artificial and lack the obvious relevance of something like "is the company making money". Two, it leads to all kinds of local optimizations where every team works for its numbers, instead of working for the big company numbers. I won't get too theoretical on this, but we'll talk about some examples in a bit.

The even bigger problem with outcome performance is that this it does not help the leader who is trying to make something work and has to make decisions now, before seeing if they are reflected, down the line, in the bottom line. The hard thing with performance is how to make hiring, promotion and organizational decisions *now* that will lead to team and organization performance at some point in the *future*.

You need to build a team and deliver a new software product: who do you hire, how do you pick, how do you organize the work?

At Endava, when I got the job to lead the Iași business unit, I had to choose my leadership team, made up, at that moment, of a Head of Development, a Head of Testing, a Head of Project Management, a Head of Architecture & Analysis and a Head of HR. We were a small business unit, around 40 people, and our biggest challenge, both in the short term and in the long term, was growth. Mature Endava business units numbered well into the hundreds and we were expected to get there as well, as fast as possible, because in the software services industry, size is everything and size is measured in number of employees. Growth meant the ability to hire people, to keep people, to organize people in teams, to deliver software services well, to work with sales to attract clients, to work with other delivery units on bigger projects. But, most of all, it meant being able to hire good people and to deliver great software. I had to pick these 5 people in a way that, together with me, would form a team that would perform, by leading the business unit to solid and healthy growth. How could I make this choice, how would I pick the right people, based on what criteria? For one, I had examples in the leadership teams of the other business units, which I knew in some detail and I could understand how they worked, what worked, what didn't, what I liked and what I didn't like about them. I also knew the other business unit managers, so I knew for example that a certain kind of head of development that worked well with business manager X wouldn't necessarily work well with me, as we had different leadership styles. The first major choice I had to make was if I was going to promote from the inside or hire from the outside. Inside we had people that were relatively junior, team lead level, two or three formal steps below these new jobs as they were seen in a mature business unit. None of them had real experience in delivering the kind of projects we were going to have to deliver and none of them had led the numbers and caliber of people they were going to have to lead. My internal candidates would have to grow really, really fast and they would have to go through a huge stretch. Hiring from the outside would have allowed me to get more experienced managers, with a proven track record of having done things like what we would have to do. Going outside would have also been the safe choice. If I was going to fail with a team of inexperienced long shots I hand picked, it was going to be my failure and mine alone. If I was going to fail after hiring people with great looking CV's, that would have been less of my failure, because I would have followed the rules. Going with the safe choice is a tried and proven corporate practice, and it was definitely something I was not going to do. In my mind, performance is not safety, nor is it predictability. Performance is change. When I was trying to think which people would perform in my team, I wasn't thinking about who was going to make the fewest mistakes, or annoy me the least, or generally be easy to work with. I was only thinking about who was going to be able to deliver the radical growth and change that I had in mind. Who was going to be willing and able to embark on such a journey? It was, first and foremost, a value thing. I felt, right or wrong, that there was, at that time, no other company in Iași like the one I wanted to build. I don't mean that we would be better in all ways than everyone else, or that everyone else sucked, no, not at all, but the kind of fanatical client obsession I wanted to have, combined with risk taking attitude of a loose, decentralized, self organizing management approach, was, I still think, at that time in Iași, pretty unique. Other experienced managers had delivered big projects in other companies, but they had done it, more often than not, in a way that was different than what I wanted to have. Sure, that didn't mean that none of the potential outside candidates would not be able to understand and rally to what we were doing, but the general premise was against it and most of the people we talked to, while good people, only convinced us that our idea of performance was, indeed, different. It was, therefore, going to be internal, because the adherence to the culture and the maniacal focus on being different was going to be, in the big scheme of things, more important than experience. I needed fanatical determination, I didn't need cold and balanced experience.

Some of the positions had clearer leading internal candidates, but some didn't. In project management for example I only had 3 PMs and they were good people, but I wanted something different for the Head of PM position so I went and offered the job to a senior developer who had no PM experience whatsoever but had what I thought were the core qualities of what a really great project manager should be, which were relentless focus on results and delivery and a flexibility in adapting and evolving along the way, combined with a natural understanding of the critical importance of communication and expectation management that I did not see in anyone else at that time. I didn't care if she could tell me what a Gantt chart was, I cared that I had seen her, again and again, never giving up, stepping in, finding a way, keeping close to the client, keeping close to the team, and that she did it in a way that you knew was in her nature. For me, performance was potential, the runway ahead. Every one of the people I chose to be in my leadership team had a list as long as my arm of things they didn't do well or things they didn't know about their new job. Any conventional, checklist based interview, would have rejected most of them. Any conventional, checklist based interview would have rejected me as well, and it almost did, as part of the internal selection process I had gone through myself. I was a college drop out. I didn't have proven experience doing what I was going to have to do. I wasn't like the other managers. I had strong opinions that I sometimes expressed in hyperbolic terms. I had little deference for authority. None of us were going to be there because we were well rounded individuals, balanced in our skills, even in our approach. I therefore made my choice and chose internally, with a vacancy for the Head of Architecture & Analysis, which we didn't have anyone ready for, nor had we any pressing need at that moment. We made the announcement, we started working, and from day one each of them started making mistakes. Was this a performance issue? Well, mostly no, because most of those mistakes were to be expected. I knew what I had chosen, I knew what they had and didn't have and I knew the gap we all had to cover as a team, myself as the leader of the team, and each of them individually. There was no point in being surprised or upset because they had trouble doing things I already knew they would struggle with. It was my job to provide an atmosphere of safety and of radical honesty, to both challenge and support, to encourage them to use their strengths, to help them fill in some of the gaps, to give them the direction they needed, in brief, to lead. On the short term, we lost some opportunities that we might have not lost with a more experienced team. On the medium and long term, I am convinced that the team shot up way and above what I could have likely gotten from the market, and did it with heart, with gusto and with the ambition only hungry people can have, because hungry we all were, hungry to do, hungry to change, hungry to prove ourselves, to each other first and foremost. Would I have been able to define, in a scorecard of some sort, using some metric or another, the kind of performance I was looking for when I was deciding what to do with this team? No. Sure, I could approximate it, and I think I even did some pros and cons analysis on the candidates, because someone asked me for it, but deep down it wasn't about a checklist: I had a story in my head, a vision of where I wanted to go, of what I wanted it to feel like, and I used my intuition, my gut feeling and my experience of working with these people to choose them based on their strengths, not their lack of weakness, and on their potential, not on their proven experience. And it was a difficult, complicated, at times headache inducing, wonderful and brilliant team, and I regret nothing.

Fast forward a decade and one the things I am now involved in these days is advising a startup that is going to have a big launch in a few months and is looking into getting a marketing person and a designer to work with them on the launch. It's going to be a significant financial risk for them to add 2 more people to the existing team of 4 and, even more important than the money, the new people need to deliver, and deliver fast. Every hour of help and coaching they need from the CEO is an hour the CEO doesn't have to work on any of the other critical things he's doing, and time is the most important commodity right now. There are several hundred precious hours of his time between now and the big day and each and every one of them matters. Clearly, he doesn't want to hire someone that is going to take the amount of work I had to put in with my team in Endava, because he doesn't have the financial nor the time luxury of investing that much in building, he needs results, and he needs them today. He is probably going to get someone that has proven experience in exactly what he needs and can hit the ground running. He may get them as contractors first and see if they can become part of the core team later. Are they going to really gel with the founders and prove to be willing and able to become part of the core team and want to be here long term? Too early to tell, too early to worry about it. For now, all this startup needs is some people to deliver on marketing and on design, quickly and effectively, and that's all that matters right now.

I have always been wary of judging performance based on numbers alone. Yes, the more senior you are, the more you need to deliver on the numbers, but I've always had a passion for the story behind the numbers. Who are you, what are you doing there, why are you doing what you're doing, what are you hoping to achieve, how are you evolving, what's getting better, what's getting worse, why, what do you need? I first and foremost look for an attitude of performance, people that care, that want to get it done. I then look for major skills or their absence and coach on that. I look for personality and what strengths and weaknesses it brings to the job. I look for intelligence. I look for determination. I look at specific situations and I look at hints about how they are likely to behave in new situations, based on how they behaved in old situations.

I hired people that had almost no experience and I rejected people with great looking CV's, because I didn't feel they had the right kind of fire in them. I hired people that were downright weird at the interview, but I thought they were the right kind of weird. I promoted people that were unsafe, that had many ways in which they could fail, but also ways in which they could shine. I tended to look for the diamond in the rough, rather than for the visible, but less precious stone. I looked for hidden strength beyond an appearance of softness and I looked for compassion beyond a front of bravado. Many of the bets I made didn't turn out to be winners. Some of the potential I thought I saw wasn't always all there. All in all, that's the nature of the game and if I had to do it again, I wouldn't be in any way more careful or more conservative: if anything, I'd move faster and bolder.

That's why it's hard for me to put performance in a matrix and that's why when you ask me why I think some person might do great, I can't easily explain it with a checklist, I have to tell you a story and you might need to trust my intuition on it. It is also totally dependent on the context and the person I would hire to lead a huge division in a big company is probably not be the person I would I like to start a business with, and viceversa.

If I had to be totally safe, if I had to cover my butt because of corporate politics and I couldn't take any chances on my people, then I would probably be forced to make all the wrong performance decisions. I am glad to have never worked in such a place and I am bent on never doing it. The freedom to bet on people being the best possible, yet unproven, version of themselves, is absolutely central to my idea of performance.

Moving on to organizational performance issues, let's look at job descriptions. Job descriptions are formal sets of qualifications, responsibilities and expected results and behaviors that are supposed to define, objectively, what a particular job is. The intentions behind job descriptions can be seen as noble, including setting clear expectations but the problem is that, like any bureaucracy left to flourish, it has gone out of control and I personally consider detailed job descriptions to be more of a problem than an asset, because the unnecessary detail changes the frame of reference from one of trust and creativity to one of zero sum negotiation. Imagine you're my buddy and I'm asking you to come pick me up from the airport and give me a ride home, help me out with that. You come, you pick me up, that helps me a bunch, I say thanks dude, I owe you one and that's it, a productive, fruitful, trustful and pleasant exchange. I gave you a job, so to say, and you did it. Now let's imagine that instead of simply asking "can you pick me up?", I would give you a detailed set of requirements on exactly how much time ahead of my landing to be there, what kind of car to bring, what kind of water to have in the car, what to wear and how to greet me when you see me. Suddenly, this is not a trustful exchange anymore, this is a detailed contract. You're not my friend, you're my Uber. You don't look like someone I can just ask something anymore, you look like someone I need to control through detailed specifications. This new dynamic will change your frame of mind too. If you're late one day and you leave me waiting, what will you do? Will you just call me and see what can be done, or will you look to protect yourself from the consequences? You'll look for the fine print in our detailed contract and find a provision saying that I need to inform you in writing 3 days or more of my exact arrival time, and you'll hope I didn't, and that will be your way out. I can't overemphasize how often that happens. Put detailed job descriptions in front of people and many of them will start going through them with a fine-tooth comb and that will change the dynamic. I've had performance reviews with people that were nowhere near ready to be promoted, I knew it, deep down they knew it, but they pulled out the job description, pointed to section 3 paragraph 12 and started arguing that, according to how they understood it, they were able to "design small to medium complexity software systems" or whatever it said there, and then we proceeded to argue, like lawyers, about the meaning of "simple" and "medium" and about what a comma meant. I stopped doing that really quickly and I don't want to ever do it again: it didn't help me, it didn't help them, and it made nothing better. Detailed job descriptions with the veneer and illusion of near perfect objectivity create a dynamic of nitpicking and of zero sum negotiation, instead of one of real feedback, of open minded conversation and of real ambition. I like clear job descriptions, I don't like detailed job descriptions, and the two are not the same. I like a good dose of objectivity and of course, I do not tolerate any kind of discrimination that has nothing to do with the actual work, but I am a big believer in subjectivity in the sense that every leader, and every team, should get to define how performance looks like for them. Let job descriptions have clear principles, highlight the key expectations, don't make detailed specifications out of them. Where things aren't clear, that is an opportunity for real conversation. The best example I know of is Ben Horowitz's "Good product manager, bad product manager" job description. It says all the important things clearly, without trying to put everything in lawyerly detail, because it's not meant to be used by idiots that don't trust each other, but by smart people that want to work together.

SMART objectives are overrated for the same reasons, because this obsession with artificial specificity and detail is counterproductive. Yes, it's important to have a clear destination and yes, sometimes a SMART approach is the right one. However, when it comes to stretch targets, when it comes to new things, forcing a measurement is counterproductive. I wanted my head of development to inspire his developers into adopting an agile ethos (this was back when adopting agile was still a thing). Should I have asked from him a specific number of presentations, training sessions, internal blog articles and what not to prove to me numerically that the did the work required to inspire developers into being agile? Or should I instead have given him a clear direction but no specific prescription and keep close to him, stay in touch, frequently talk, mostly just talk, about how it was going, what he tried, what he found out, what worked, what didn't? I chose the latter and I think you should too.

The yearly performance evaluation cycle is a disaster. Twice a year is half the disaster. In these kind of cycles as they're usually done, managers are not close enough to their people and do not give continuous, frequent, Radically Honest feedback. Time then comes, once or twice a year, to measure performance and, frequently, decide reward based on it. Managers gather feedback retroactively and the entire company halts as forms of all sort are filled. Poison fills the hallways as everyone worries and stresses and prepares to make their case. Old emails are dug up and dusted. Vague memories are resurrected. The managers know in their guts who did well and who didn't, but they have to justify it in corporate speak, so they do. They find that one instance when, back in November, the person did something wrong. Why that instance and not another? Because there's an email about this one and they can point to something specific, and they found nothing written about all the other instances. The employee comes with the job description and engages in a text analysis of what performance means. Should he, at his level of seniority, according to section B paragraph 6 of the job description, do that at all? It's an accounting conversation, not a performance conversation. It's a cold, wet mess that nobody comes out of feeling good. Expectations are not aligned and there is no way to win when this happens. If the employee was expecting a raise and you don't give him one, even if you manage to somehow convincingly "prove" to him that he didn't really deserve it, that will not make him happy, and it will still leave a bitter taste. He came in with an expectation, with a view of himself, and you sent him away feeling worse about his own performance. If he wasn't doing well, why didn't you tell him in time, so he could change? That is a valid question. Why bring up that November email now, in June, why didn't you bring it up in November, so he could do something about it?

If you have to have a yearly formal evaluation, turn it into a formality. Have continuous real CRH feedback every day and have real, monthly, 1-1s, such that when the formal yearly checkup comes, nobody has any unrealistic expectations, everyone already knows where they stand. The 1-1 meetings should not be status meetings and managers should not hide behind process, or formality, by ticking boxes or tracking objectives, just to keep the conversation safely flowing. This is the meeting where the most difficult things should be addressed. The most important things managers need to do in this meeting is listen, observe, shut up and ask the right questions, no matter how difficult they may be. You need to know where your people stand, and they need to know where you're standing. There should be no doubt in their heads of how you see them and their performance and you should have no doubt in yours about how they see their situation, their work and their career.

The most important thing you can do to have the right performance culture is to have frequent, monthly at most, real 1-1s, using Compassionate Radical Honesty. Obsess about this, this is 90% of what matters. Add clear but ambitious job descriptions, similar to the Good Product Manager / Bad Product Manager example above.

How do you know when you have it, how do you define success? Like justice Stewart said, you'll know it when you see it. You'll know.

What about stack ranking, the idea of having mandated percentages of your people that you consider the best, ok and the worst. I'm against it. Don't get me wrong, I want each and every one of my managers to be able to honestly and straightforwardly explain at any moment who's doing how in their team and who are their best people, and I want them to act where action is needed. However, forcing them to fire the bottom x%, or forcing them to distribute rewards in fixed percentages across the categories, I dislike the rigidity of that approach. For one, performance is contextual and not all people are the same. Not all members of the team are comparable to each other directly. Second, some people are not superstars, always growing or doing something new, but are rock solid, stable performers. Should you fire them or never reward them? No, I don't think so. Neither am I an adept of the opposite approach of giving a little to everyone, so nobody gets upset. I always asked my managers to reward disproportionately and be brave in doing so, but I wanted them to use their judgement for it, not some Gauss curve of some sort. That made my work harder, because I needed better managers, but that's how I liked it.

When it comes to objectivity vs subjectivity, I am a big believer in manager discretion to choose her team. She has to do it fairly, transparently, clearly, in a way that is in the interest of the company as a whole, 100% ethically, but she gets to choose her team and I would never want to see a manager forced to work with someone they don't want in their team, because I trust my managers, and the moment I stop trusting them, they are not my managers anymore. When it comes to performance evaluation, there is a part of the evaluation that is objective, and it has to be, but a part of it is subjective and I really value that part as well. The only thing I tell my managers is to not do is to never hide behind a veneer of objectivity, because then it's going to be bullshit. Say it clearly. Say what you expect, you, as the individual manager. I need people on my team that I can communicate with easily, that I gel with, that understand the value of the team, that we understand each other, and all these things matter to me. If you are an otherwise excellent professional with bullet proof hard skills and disciplined delivery, but we have no chemistry, then I do not want you in my team, and it's not your fault, and I'm sure you'll do great in another team.

What is the relationship between performance and compensation? In purely economic terms, none. The price of talent, salary + benefits, is driven by market dynamics such as supply and demand. That one gray haired Cobol developer over there in the corner, quietly working on an equally gray haired code base, might be paid three times as much as the brilliant front end architect over here, because he's the only Cobol developer left in the Eastern hemisphere and we really need him. This has nothing to do with his performance and we are not saying that he's three times as good of a Cobol developer as this other guy is a front end architect. All we're saying is that that's his market price and that someone, some client, is willing to pay us sufficiently for him, directly or indirectly. Now, the fact that pure economics says this doesn't mean that this should automatically be your compensation policy. You could go solely on market price, but then you'd have to clearly communicate it as such and that would drive some people away, attract other and would lead to a certain culture that you may or may not want. If I'm thinking about Iași, of Romania, we need more management and leadership transparency on this, as the market dynamics and the economic perspective are not discussed and acknowledge enough. Market value, in the long run, is always going to determine the majority of the compensation. If skill X is paid half as much as skill Y, you will end up, on average, paying for X people about as half as for Y people, trust me. You can't fight the market. However, what do you do when you compare two X people, who do you pay more? Ideally, you should look at the value they bring to the business, in terms of stuff delivered, of actual contribution. You are therefore, in a sense, and within a range (explicit or not), paying for performance, but performance understood as much as possible as real value. You're not paying because they know how to write good code, you're paying them because they actually write the right code for you and by that add value to your business. The reason you're paying your better people more is because you want to keep them happy, because if they're unhappy they will leave. You're also operating in a competitive market and if your people are underpaid in relation to market value, they are easier to poach. That's why you're paying your fast trackers even more, because you're not paying for their value right now, you're paying for their value averaged over 18 months or so, and their value will increase quickly. Where it gets distorted and confusing is that many people think they should be paid for effort. Effort deserves to be recognized and it's part of what it means to be a good professional, but effort in and by itself has no market value. Results have market value. Make the distinction clear. You're looking for results, not work. You will appreciate work, you will demand work, but results are the ultimate goal. Skill and effort are necessary precursors to results, but they are not, strictly speaking, results.

Whatever you choose as your compensation policy, you should do three things:

1. Clearly communicate it, own it, make it transparent, make it well known and understood by all. Compensation through obscurity, hoping to keep people content by having them not know how you make decisions and how you treat them in relation to their colleagues, is a fool's game.
2. Make it fair. Whatever it is, it is the same for all and everyone has equal opportunity, within the constraints of what the market allows.
3. Make it apolitical, make it simple, make it easy to understand.

All this and more, however you choose to have it, is your performance story and your performance story is a big part of our culture story. You need to talk about what performance means in your company, you need to highlight examples, to reward publicly, to create a lore around it. Everyone in your team needs to know what performance is and how performance looks like. Performance is not a taboo subject, from the contrary, it has to be one of the most discussed things in your team and in your company, at all levels and it all corners.

Changing hearts and minds

Whenever you talk about something or you do something, your end goal is to change the hearts and mind of those around you, so the next time they know how to do it well, without you having to be around. You are not simply speaking the truth because it is true, you are also speaking it to educate. Impact and change are the end game. You don't distort the truth, you don't manipulate, but you do choose what to focus on at any given moment, you don't simply open your mouth and start talking whatever you feel like at the moment, because you are not a child. You are deliberate, as a leader you have to be deliberate.

If you, for example, inherit a demotivated, disruptive team and you want to shape them up and make them perform, you will give them feedback about their performance, you will make your expectations clear, you will demand new behaviors and new results of them. Once you do that, for a while they will make so many mistakes that you will be justified, technically speaking, to criticize them 10 times a day if you so wished, and your criticism will be true, you will be speaking the truth, but will you be changing hearts and minds? Are you making them better, are you getting them on your side, are you fixing the situation, or are you just letting steam off, feeling good that you are telling it to them like it is? What is your long game, where do you want to take them?

Most of what you say in terms of feedback will be in the hope of changing hearts and minds. Some of it will be just information for them to do whatever with it, but the important things will be about building a certain kind of team, and that is usually deliberate feedback. There is spontaneity in it, as in it's not all planned in detail, you also react, and that's fine, but the overall direction is deliberate.

Extraordinary teams in average locations?

You won't have access to the best people, by whatever definition you want to use, there will always be some, somewhere else, better. You won't have the most money, the best location or the best information. You yourself are not the best, you personally know people that are better than you and you can only imagine how many more of them there are out there in this big world of ours.

How can you compete? How can you do something truly outstanding when you don't have the best at your disposal? There are three parts to this answer.

The first part is that, for some things, you can't compete. If you want to build the best jet fighter plane in Iași, you won't. There's just too much required to even start on something like that, too much ecosystem, too many dependencies that you can't even begin to hope to have over here.

The second part is that, for more and more things, you can compete. The internet, software, it's all leveled the playing field to a degree previously unimaginable for most of our history so far. Is it all level and equal? Hell no, and it never will be. But you do have a real shot, provided you choose the right arena to get into.

And the third thing is the magic of teams. Groups of people, when becoming a real team, dedicated, determined, hungry, can succeed where others have failed, even though others were better qualified and had many more resources at their disposal. It happens all the time. It is the innovator's dilemma, it is the attacker's advantage, it's luck, it's determination, it's obsession, it's all of the above, but it happens.

Stop worrying. Stop idolizing. Admire, respect, pick your battles and go all in. Destroy your idols, that's the best way to show your respect.

Step 7: The magic

You don't have a lot of time

Whatever you do, do it like it needs to happen today, because you don't have a lot of time, and I'm not even talking about life and philosophy. Every job comes with an expiration date and you have a window of a year, a couple of years at most, to figure out what that job is about and what is it that you want to do with it other than just cruising along. You then have a few more years to make your mark, before the opportunity passes and it's time to either reinvent your job or move on. Your whole career is going to have just several of these cycles and you have to get the most out of them, for your personal and professional betterment. Don't waste your time.

For the past year and a half at my last corporate job, I was already thinking about going out on my own. I was, at least weekly, putting deliberate time into imagining what I'd like to do after I left. I had many ideas sketched, some with business plans attached. The problem was, the more this potential future took shape in my head, the less urgency to actually do something I felt. I was feeling good simply because I was investing intellectual and emotional energy into picturing what I might do. The thinking itself seemed like a sufficient achievement, it relaxed me, made me complacent and I was living the illusion that thinking is the same as doing. It is not. Days, weeks and months passed, and still I would do nothing to bring the future I wanted even one inch closer. Overall, I loved that job, but I should have stayed for 5 years, not 7. After 5, I had done what I had set out to do and I wasn't finding something new to engage in, to reinvent myself, to attack with the same passion as before. I should have left then and there, but I was too comfortable, I hung around, I lingered, competent, but bored and getting nowhere. I won't make this mistake again and neither should you.

What are you going to do today to get you closer to your dream? Not preparation for what you are going to do tomorrow, not planning for what you are going to do a week from now, but what are you actually going to do today? Get something from each day, extract profit before every sunset, be it in money, in wisdom, in relationships or, better still, in all of them.

The time to start is now, and the time to stop may also be now. Let go of the past and get started with the future. Start now. The best time is, always, now. Make today count and tomorrow will be that much closer to your current destination.

Am I saying that I always avoid a lifelong perspective, that I never think long term? No, I do, of course I do, but there's only so much of that kind of thinking you can engage in before it turns useless. How much do you need to spend picturing your distant future, how much can you really plan 20 years in advance, before it turns into unproductive day dreaming and the real question moves to what are you going to do today? Think in decades, by all means, but soon enough, you will end up right back where you started from: what matters most is right now.

You really, really, don't have a lot of time. You come to work early in the morning, blink twice, and it's time to go home. Days and years add up just like that. Get something from today, don't let it bullshit you that tomorrow is when you get yours.

Lead everything

I was running in this mountain race a couple of months back, and I was closing in on a checkpoint, a couple of hundred meters ahead. Just behind me there was a girl and a few more steps behind her, a guy, a turtle looking dude, one of those runners equipped with half the running store on him: black headband, black gloves, sunglasses, knee and elbow protection, water pipe coming out of his backpack, the works. As we get close to the checkpoint, we see there was someone there filming, had a camera on a gimbal and started running alongside us, to get a nice tracking shot as we passed by. Suddenly, as soon as he saw the camera, the turtle looking guy sprinted in the front our little pack, in my face, locked in on a double thumbs up and started showing off to the camera. He had been very comfortable at the back for the past couple of miles, but now he had to be in the front. When I say "lead everything", that is not what I mean. Don't be the turtle looking guy.

Whatever you do, do it deliberately. You don't have to lead everything in the sense of taking charge, of being in control of every initiative you're part of, but you have to always lead yourself. Why are you there? What are you doing? Who expects what from you? How can you deliver? Understand, manage, own and lead all these things. Own your existence, be deliberate, understand what you're doing. There's nothing wrong with playtime, but even then, you know that is what you're doing.

Don't stay in places where you don't want to be, feeling bad and complaining all the time. What are you doing there, wasting your life? The only valid answer for being in a place you hate is if you really, but really, don't have any other option. Change it or leave it. Otherwise, you are complicit to your own misery and you are not leading yourself.

You are responsible for your own life and feelings so start acting like it.

Wherever you are, do your best. If the client difficult? Great, get better at dealing with them, learn something new while at it. Is the team demotivated? Great, get better at motivating them, learn how to do that. Do you have a small budget? Great, learn to get by with little. These are not problems, these are the steps of becoming. Do your best. Keep at it. When you need help, ask for it, don't wait and hope it will fall out of the sky. When you want to leave, leave, but leave like a pro, don't run. You are either getting somewhere, or you're not. If you're stuck and your decision is to turn into a passive aggressive, gossiping, lazy, reactive, no good complainer, you've just made a mockery of your own potential.

I'm not telling you all this thinking that I have all the answers, because I don't. I don't know your struggles. Whatever I managed to overcome and get done I did in my circumstances, which are different from yours. I worked hard, yes, but I have no simplistic illusion that whatever worked for me will magically work for you. Your struggle is your own, but what I am saying to you is this: strength is better than weakness and, unless you're a narcissistic psychopath, and you likely aren't, then you are very likely stronger than you think you are. Find that strength. I've told you some of the things I did so you can take as example. I was also lucky to have a few people around me that gave me that helping hand when I needed it the most, and you may have some too. That having been said, it's wise to act like the only help you can always rely on is the help you are able and willing to give yourself.

Don't waste your time, don't waste other people's time, and don't squander your potential. Find your strength, lead yourself.

Don't be a good worker

Rebellion is a tricky thing to get right, so hard to do when you really need it, and so easy to do when it's really nothing special. The world is full of both shallow rebels that take themselves too seriously, and of obedient, compliant workers that should, at least once in a while, just stop doing what they're told.

One of the most natural and saddest processes in all of human society is the collapse, with the onset of adulthood, of the seemingly wide ranging potential of the youth into one predictable life path. I remember, alongside me, throughout my school years, many other kids speaking about how they were not going to play the game, how they were going to be something else, do something else, how they were going to change things. In time, one by one, the vast majority of them folded into the mainstream, transformed into good workers and average citizens. Some of you might see this process as a positive, the civilizing force, society's ability to integrate its new generations and make them productive, reliable, contributing members of the whole. I see that too, and I get it, but it still saddens me. I am in that sense unadjusted and probably absurd, but that is the only way in which I know how to be. I am unrealistic in expectations, prone to complicate my life, eager to fight for ideals, to go against the norm, to rock the boat, because that's what I do, and I'd be so much less without it, so I ask that from you too, because I think there are more of us then we sometimes fear.

I am not telling you to be unpredictable for the sake of being unpredictable and I'm definitely not telling you to be capricious, but I am telling you that doing what you're told, being a good boy, being a good girl, that's not all it's cracked up to be. The machine is going to suck you up and turn your soul into societal paste. Be mischievous once in a while, set something on fire, push something to the limit and beyond, try something outrageous, push some people way more than you or they thought possible, break yourself trying the impossible, upset things, get people to envy you, to be jealous of you, slam a door, love or crush your enemy and dance under the moonlight. Be whatever you once dreamed you could, fail trying, become something else, get off the boring bus and run into the wild.

Ultimate professional relationships

If you were to wake up in a ditch outside the city, all bruised and hurting, not remembering how you got there, who would you call first?

In my case, family aside, it would be one of 4 or 5 very close business partners. Why not a friend? Because I don't have any better friend than these people, although they themselves are not quite friends. Let me explain.

In my work, I frequently get asked the following question: "Is it ok to develop friendships with colleagues and clients?", and I usually have a tough time answering it, because I don't see professional relationships and friendship as two completely different paths. It's easy to give some practical advice, such as not getting too familiar too early with your client and not getting wasted during the company party with the CEO watching you trying to drink from three beer bottles at once, but that's just the surface of it and there's something more important to explore here.

The people I am closest to, outside family, are people I've met and got to know through working with them on something of consequence, be it business, or some other kind of initiative. It's that way I've got to know them for years and that's how trust was built. We know each other's values, we know our musical and literary preferences, we know our politics, we debate Star Wars vs Star Trek, we know what we're good at, what we're bad at, we have no secrets and we feel very comfortable and safe in each other's presence. The vast majority of the time we've ever spent together was around the work we did, on a project, building something, having some beers after. We don't go out for barbecues, we don't spend weekends together, it was years before we met our each other's significant others, and if we go together on a trip of some sort, more likely than not, it's a business trip. Our friendship has evolved from our work and is grounded in our work.

I call these ultimate professional relationships. You could call them friendships, and that wouldn't be totally wrong, but it would be insufficient, and it would be missing the point. There is a kind of connection you develop with your true partners that is stronger and better than mere friendship. We feel best when we meet to do something. It's a friendship of action, friendship with content.

I don't know how to have friends that I share no passion with, that I share no work with, but I do know how to have the friends I have, and I'm very grateful for them.

Legacy

Do everything for legacy, and do nothing for legacy. Do everything with the intent of leaving everything better than you found it, of helping people be better, but understand that things, and people, you included, get forgotten easily. If your drive is glory, then make sure you understand what glory is so you're not disappointed by it when you get it. If you're drive is, like some psychologists say, a desire to achieve a sort of immortality through what you leave behind, I'm not going to tell you that's wrong, but I would recommend that you also understand that you are going to die and that your legacy is going to follow soon after.

Bill Hewlett and David Packard were, to Steve Job's generation, the original Silicon Valley icons and role models, and the company they founded, HP, a shining light of innovation and good management. Fast forward 40 years, HP is a pale shadow of its former self, inspiration to no one, Bill and David passed and cvasi forgotten, their names and leadership examples on nobody's lips anymore. Just these days I was chatting with some friends about Evernote, a few years ago an example of the little startup that could, a good idea well executed, with a bit of a cult following and a reasonably large number of hard-core fans, a company often given as a positive example just yesterday it seems. We were observing that we haven't heard anything about it recently and that we hadn't used its product in a long time. A quick google and the first news result I get about it is that it's in a "death spiral". I hope that's not true, but even so, compared to HP, Evernote feels like a flash in the pan and yet, for a few years at least, its founder and CEO must have felt like being on top of the world. Henry Ford is a longer lasting icon, still quoted to this day, 4-5 generations after his time. *"If I had asked people what they wanted, they would have said faster horses"* he famously declared. And yet, the Ford Motor Company that he left behind is no leader of the automobile industry and hasn't been one for a long time. They haven't innovated or changed anything major since Henry's time and they are, at the time of writing this, perilously sliding into even more irrelevance and potential bankruptcy. They may survive, as they have in the past, but I can tell you nobody's quoting today's Ford or its CEO, whoever he or she may be. So much for legacy.

And yet, is what Henry Ford did meaningless? Is Bill and David's work all lost because the current version of HP is a laggard? Should we criticize Evernote that they even tried? No, no and not at all. Regardless of what happens to the Ford company, Henry Ford's impact and vision was already realized the moment he helped usher in the automobile age. Regardless of where HP ends up, Bill and David's legacy has already been realized through their innovations, their contribution to the valley and their mentorship and inspiration to the next generation of entrepreneurs that went on to move the world forward. Evernote tried and reached farther than 99.999% of us do and in the process made some clients happy, solved some problems and employed some good people. That is real legacy too. Nothing lasts forever, nothing really lasts very long at all, but, in its way, everything matters.

I have this dear friend of mine and he plays and sings in a band. He is reasonably successful and has his dedicated fans, but no stardom yet, no throngs of teenagers mobbing him for an autograph when he goes to the mall. He may still get that, and that would make me very happy, but even if he doesn't, does that mean that his music so far is a failure? The exact opposite is true. It is beautiful, honest music, crafted from the heart, that has touched and made better the lives of many, that has given people moments of joy, moments of peace, that has comforted pain and has enriched the lives of others and, in the end, what more can you ask for?

Do I hope that I will someday do something worthy enough that people will mention me for something I did? Of course I do, I try to think as big as I can and do as much as I am able, within the limits of the kind of life that I choose to lead. Will I get there? I don't know. Will my life be wasted if I don't? Not for me. I aim for the stars, but I know the stars are very far away. I want to be one in a million and I might do it, but I also try to have the humility to understand that, in the end, even that won't make me special, it's just a numbers game. Why do I do it then? I do it because it's fun, it feels much better than not trying, and I do it because I want to build something, and I want to make the world just a tiny bit better.

It's a tricky thing this desire for legacy. It can give you the fire you need, or it can burn you. It can make you sad and it can intoxicate you with overconfidence. Whatever you choose to do, make sure to leave things around you just a bit better than what you found and that is, in my book, a life lived well and a life worth living.

The time to be an optimist is now

Every step of the way, there is no shortage of disappointment and pain to drag you down. Even absent real tragedy, you will always have to contend with the host of daily frustrations and disillusions, the thousand little cuts of life taking its toll.

The people you work with will be capable of wonderful deeds but also of bitterly letting you down. There will be days when you will look back on your years of work and suddenly feel the November wind blowing through their emptiness, unable to muster any convincing answer to the question of why are you doing all this? What are you really changing? Nothing, will snap the biting answer, your own mind turning on you, ready to pour salt in your existential wound, and you will feel like all you want to do is crawl into a corner and be very, very quiet.

My biggest professional doubt is about the impact I'm really having, or not. There are times, there are interactions, there are moments when the result of my work is evident, and I can clearly see the good I manage to do, the change I trigger. There are people telling me this, I can see it in their eyes, I can see it in their actions, and that is the sunny side of my work, always balanced by the near infinite size of what I didn't yet do and I what never will, because of human nature, because of the complexity and magnitude of the world, because of how small I am in this big universe of ours, because of how hard everything can be.

Just the other day I met with someone and his hand was shaking as he was raising the coffee cup to his lips, overwhelmed by the big worries of where is the world going, what's happening with us, the political developments, the damage we're doing to the environment. Accurate or not in his assessment, he was carrying the weight of the world on his shoulders, condemning himself to certain failure, because when you worry about things of such magnitude, in this corrosive way, there is no winning. Worry of this nature subdues you, frightens you, paralyzes you, keeps you awake at night, makes you feel like you'd be engaging in an act of treason if you were to worry just a bit less and do just a bit more, makes it feel like some kind of sin if you were to allow yourself some joy. Worry of this kind is the insidious trap of pessimism paralyzing you from taking any action. Worry of this nature doesn't help you do your part, does not help you contribute, it only makes you afraid. I know, I've been there.

The little things can trip you up too. An unexpected hurdle too early in the morning, someone making the same silly mistake for the umpteenth time, dropping your phone on the sidewalk and seeing it crack, these things, superficial as they are, can ruin your whole day and instantly drain your enthusiasm, leaving you to wonder how real it was anyway, if it all it took to sap it was something small like that. Where is your resilience? You now doubt yourself.

Faced with such dilemmas, big and small, I and you, we have two easy roads in front of us that we could take. We also have a third road, and this third way is the hard way, but the right way.

The first easy road is the road of eternal disappointment, of sadness, of despair, of persistent pessimism. It is a hard road to be on, but it is easy to take and it's easy to make a case for it, because all you have to do is imagine the vastness of space and time, see yourself as a little powerless and meaningless ant and you're done, case closed, nothing is worth it. The vastness of humanity's failures, collective or individual, evil or merely incompetent, stupid or malicious, is equally overwhelming. Looked at in a certain way, the road of despair is the only logical choice, but it's a trap.

The other easy road to take is the way of rowdy unproven confidence, of facile cheerfulness, of the eternal smile, the hollow sounding excessive positivity, detached from any kind of complexity, from any trace of sophistication, unreal, untested, incapable of a certain kind of contemplation. I've been there too, and I was there because of how my brain worked, through an excess of positivity neurotransmitters, and because I had not yet failed in a way that made me stop and understand myself. It was not deep confidence, it was cockiness. In a way it worked, because displays of self confidence tend to work, but it worked on a surface level, playing at a game I did not know the true depths of.

Pain is part of who I am, and pain is part of who you are and if you don't know it yet, you will. Pain does not need to be ignored, pain does not need to be eliminated, pain intertwines with joy and a million other things and out of it comes life. True leaders are not focused on not feeling any pain, on not having any doubt, on not experiencing any darkness, in themselves and in others. True leaders do not wallow in pain and do not fall prey to persistent, contagious pessimism, but they do not ignore it either. Meaningful optimism does not come out of simply feeling good, out of having never failed, or out of avoiding your darkest fears at all costs, until you almost fool yourself into thinking they are not there anymore. Meaningful optimism can only exist after having faced the abyss and having made the choice that your life is worth living and that your work is worth doing. After you've made the choice to care, and it can only be a choice, because there is no way to demonstrate the meaningfulness of who you are and what you do, then and only then meaningful optimism becomes possible. The other option you have is to delegate the choice that you should care to some third party, real or imaginary, divine or earthly, if you can't or don't want to make it on your own authority, by yourself and for yourself. I have a strong preference for the former.

The choice to care, the third way, the leader's way, the road of meaningful optimism.

The optimist, having decided to give a damn, about herself and about the world, is now going to start looking for ways to make herself better, to improve herself, and to make her surroundings better. His ambition, his scope, is going to vary and depend on his perceived internal strength, on his context and on his means. Some will aim to change the world, some will start by cleaning their room. Some will work to cure cancer, some will start by smiling to their neighbor. I never judge anyone on the magnitude of the good they are trying to do, the only thing anyone can really ask of any of us is to try a little bit more today than we tried yesterday, to not leave ourselves underutilized and to not waste our capacity for change.

Optimism is not just one big choice you make once on the overall direction of your life, it's many, daily choices. Do you decide to invest time and energy in improving something at work, because that's going to make you better and is going to make some small part of some system better, or do you decide to be a pessimist and say whatever, who cares anyway? Are you going to voluntarily take the time to teach someone a better way, or are you going to stay in your corner, because it's not your job to care about it? Are you, like in the old fable, going to be one of the many awkwardly stepping around the big stone left in the middle of the road, or are you going to stop and drag it to the side, improving the situation for yourself and everyone else? Do you take the couple of minutes a week you need to put your plastic in a separate bag and take it to the right bin, or are you saying to yourself that what's the point, your little bag of plastic is just a drop in the ocean anyway? Are you going to give the smile, do the act of kindness right in front of you, or are you going to reject it? Are you going to find reasons to be bitter, inactive and passive, because why should anything start with you, why should you be the first to do some good, after all, when did you ever sign up to be a good deed maker, right? Are you going to be a pessimist and find reasons at every step to stay out of it, to not do it, to not improve anything, to just mind your business, to focus on the minimal possible routine of your life, because deep down you value your own actions so little that you do not think they can make a difference, no matter how small? Pessimism is selling yourself short, pessimism is lack of self-respect, pessimism is lack of self-worth, pessimism is the belief that your actions and words don't matter, so you end up not doing much at all. Optimism is the opposite. Optimism is the belief that what you do matters.

The time to be an optimist is now, because the time to be an optimist is all the time. Meaningful optimism is a choice you have to make because nobody else can make it for you. Free people, people that stand on their own in the world, free people have to decide what they want to do with their life, such as it may be, and my decision, and my advice to you, is to decide on optimism.

Life is just too short for anything else.

www.ingramcontent.com/pod-product-compliance
Lightning Source LLC
Chambersburg PA
CBHW031620210526
45464CB00004B/1663